A NEW INTRODUCTION TO
journalism

Graham Greer

Juta & Co, Ltd

First published 1999

© Juta & Co. Ltd 1999
PO Box 14373, Kenwyn 7790

ISBN 0 7021 4374 X

Printed and bound in South Africa by Creda Communications, Eliot Avenue, Epping Industria II, Cape Town.

Contents

Foreword

This is a book for all who wish to become journalists. Those who wish to go out and seek stories and present them to their audience. Journalism is an exciting and rewarding profession. To become a good journalist is challenging and requires hard work and dedication.

The original idea for this book came from the fact that the majority of the journalism students in South Africa today, are English second language learners. Unfortunately, most of the journalism textbooks available, with one notable exception, are either from the USA or the United Kingdom and not accessible for these learners.

With particular encouragement from Prof John van Zyl and Brian Wafawarowa of Juta & Co I set off writing this text which I hope has an African feel to it so that all journalism students from our continent can identify with it. The examples used and the journalists mentioned are well-known to South African learners.

Writing the text was the easy part, but ensuring that the text was accessible to all was left to editor Jane Jackson who brought her particular precise style and considerable expertise to the text.

I hope this book will play some part in helping aspirant journalists achieve their goals of joining the 'Fourth Estate'.

Graham Greer

The Team

Author: *Graham Greer* lectures journalism in the Department of Public Relations and Journalism at the M L Sultan Technikon. His particular interest is journalism education. He started his journalism career in the industrial press and has published, written and edited industrial, sport and social awareness publications.
Graham is an executive member of, and represents journalism educators and trainers on, the National Standards Body for Communication and Language Studies. He has been a freelance feature writer for the *Natal Witness* and is currently a theatre critic for the *Sunday Tribune* in Durban. Graham also has extensive experience in both advertising and public relations.

Editor: *Jane Jackson* has worked as a language teacher, reporter, editor of *Grocott's Mail*, teacher trainer and researcher and writer of educational materials for teachers and learners in a variety of settings. She is currently employed by an inservice teacher development agency, and is involved in teacher training and curriculum design, and in developing, writing and editing materials for teachers and learners.

Designer: *Mthandeni Zama* completed his design diploma in 1997 at the M L Sultan Technikon. In that year he was awarded by the *Mail & Guardian* the Design Student of the Year. Mthandeni was sponsored for his studies by the Advertising and Design Corporation and now works as a designer for the Flagship Group.

Acknowledgements

There are so many people to thank, who all assisted in some way, in the writing of this book. If I forget anyone please forgive me.

To my inspiration – Haj Vahed and my sons Sean and Lyle, who put up with the long hours I locked myself away with this 'baby'.

To the instigator – Prof John van Zyl without whose encouragement I do not think I would have attempted this project.

To my publisher – Brian Wafawarowa – a writer's dream.

To my editor – Jane Jackson – whose expertise was invaluable.

To Mthandeni Zama who was responsible for the brilliant cover design, icons and the drawings.

To my contributors – Derrick Alberts, Fiona Cook, Marlan Padayachee, Sam Sole, and Graham Addison.

To the following final year students who contributed to Chapter 15 – Salma Patel, Sandra Mokoka, Ncumisa Fandesi, Jillian Green, Ronda Naidu, Shona Terri Naidoo, Nevenka Chitray, Lawrence Mfeka, Xolani Luthuli, Goodman Msomi, Khulekani Zuma, Moses Shiba, Sisa Qaba, Sureshnie Govender, Jennene Singh, Devendhree Perumal and Nirosha Naidoo.

To Shamolia Naidu who gave up her time to research each chapter so thoroughly.

To my colleagues in the department for giving me the encouragement and the space to complete this book.

To the *Sunday Tribune*, Vasantha Angamuthu and Grant Erskine for the kind permission to use all the photos in Chapter 16.

To the journalism students of the M L Sultan Technikon for their enthusiasm and preparedness to pilot each chapter and to offer their constructive criticism. Without their co-operation the writing of this book would have been impossible.

And finally to all the journalists, editors, fellow teachers, colleagues and friends whose advice and practice have inspired and guided me, thank you.

To the Learner

You will probably read this book as part of a course which introduces you to the study and practice of journalism. It is therefore designed to give you a broad picture of the career you have chosen. It is also a workbook as much as a textbook. As a reporter you must be ready to think fast and clearly so that you can make decisions and take action on a story. The book takes a practical approach to help you develop these skills.

You will see that every chapter includes *5 Minute Tasks* and *10 Minute Tasks*. Some tasks appear at the beginning of a chapter or at the beginning of a section. These tasks should help you to read on with understanding. They encourage you to develop your own ideas or questions and to make a mental map of the topic you are going to read about.

The tasks at the end of a chapter should help you to review what you have read and develop a clear overview of the chapter in your mind.

It is up to you and your lecturer whether you do the tasks or not. But as you will see, many of the tasks ask you to use actual newspapers in different ways, such as comparing their style or appearance with other newspapers, etc. These tasks will help you to get a more practical understanding of what you are reading and studying. You should keep a supply of past editions of various newspapers so that you can do the tasks. This should be quite easy to organise.

Several tasks ask you to consider what you know about a topic already. Remember that your knowledge and experience is important, however small it may seem to you. It can form a starting-block for what you are going to learn.

Some of the tasks suggest that you work in a group or in pairs. This is just so that you can share knowledge and ideas with others, to direct your reading and study more effectively. But you can still gain from such a task if you do it by yourself.

Don't worry if tasks take more or less time than they are supposed to. The time allocated is just a guide. Do the tasks in the way that suits you.

This book has been edited to make it readable for students of all language backgrounds, as long as they have a fair command of English. Because some English words or expressions may be difficult for some readers, there are explanations in square brackets [ ] after these words or expressions.

The book includes many quotations from journalists or writers about journalism, as well as quotes from newspaper stories, and so on. All such quotes are in italics. Italics have also been used for special terms or concepts that you need to understand in any topic.

So, you want to be a
1   journalist?

Introduction

So, you want to be a journalist? You may already have many ideas about what a journalist's work is like. This chapter will help you to examine your ideas and check them against the reality. Journalism will demand hard work and dedication from you. At first it may seem much less glamorous than you expected. However, it will bring you opportunities to meet a great variety of people, witness important events, and even make a difference to people's lives.

Outcome

At the end of this chapter, you will understand what journalism is, what a journalist does and what personal qualities you require to become a journalist.

What is journalism?

A definition of journalism is: *the profession or practice of reporting about, photographing, or editing news stories for one of the mass media.* But what are mass media? They can be defined as *those means of communication that reach large numbers of people, such as television, radio, newspapers and magazines.* Nowadays mass media also include the World Wide Web (WWW), i.e. the Internet.

A journalist is therefore a person who reports about, photographs or edits news stories for one or more of these mass media: radio, television, newspapers, magazines or the WWW.

As I have already mentioned in the preface, in this book the focus will be mainly on print media and on newspapers in particular. Because this is an *introduction* to newspaper journalism, the book focuses on news reporting rather than articles that require or demand the writer's opinion. Only much later in your journalistic career will you be allowed to write articles in which you may express your opinion. Reporting, as you will soon learn, is about being impartial and objective and reporting the facts.

5 Minute Task

> Jot down your first, honest responses to the following
> two questions:
> • Why do you want to become a journalist?
> • What do you think a journalist's life is like?
> Now read on and see if your ideas match the ideas below.

What is a journalist's life really like?

Many people decide to become journalists because their high
school teachers tell them that they are good at writing. Others
choose journalism because they wish to make the world a better
place to live in. Some believe that as journalists they will meet
important, exciting people and travel to far-away, exotic places.
There are also those who believe that their writing or broadcasting
will make them famous.

Real journalists are usually very different from these 'dream' journalists.
Yes, journalism is one of the most exciting professions, but it is also
very demanding. It takes long hours of planning, research and
checking facts. It is true that our work can make a difference to
people's lives, but to do so, we have to be accurate and dedicated.
Only those who are ready to work long hours will survive and
succeed as journalists, because journalism is not an eight to five job.
The news never stops.

The very best journalists have such a strong curiosity and interest that
they can write about anything. Journalists must be active listeners and
careful observers. They must be able to see further than those things
which are easily seen and understood; that is, they must read
between the lines.

Journalism does have some special advantages as a profession.
Firstly, you can be useful to your community and society by showing
what is really happening there; and at the same time you can get
fun and personal fulfilment from the work.

As a journalist, you will get the chance to play roles such as detective, lawyer, teacher or critic and actually get paid for doing so. Sometimes this work will get results and make a difference to people's lives. Very few journalists have ever brought down a corrupt government as a whole, or exposed fraud on a national scale. But many have indeed managed, through their reporting, to get laws changed and wrongs righted. For example, large companies have recalled faulty products or improved bad service after exposure in the media.

Further, as a journalist, you get paid to witness some of the most important and exciting events in the world, such as the inauguration of a president. You may also witness some terrible tragedies such as famines and wars. Your task will then be to make people fully aware of what is happening.

Now that you have some impression of the work and the qualities needed, what will it be like getting there? As in all professions, you have to study and work your way up from the bottom. To become a good journalist you must practise what you have learned. At first you will make mistakes, but you should accept these as part of your learning process. You will make progress by learning from your mistakes and learning to take both good and bad criticism. Some people may dislike what you have written and disagree with it. You may learn a lot from examining their views.

What qualifications will you need to get a job? This can vary, but a beginner without a university degree or a journalism diploma will certainly find it very difficult to find a job with a major newspaper.

Finally, will you make a lot of money as a journalist? You will never get really rich by being a newspaper or magazine reporter but you will have one of the most interesting and fulfilling careers that anyone can ask for.

What skills and abilities will make you a good journalist?

As a student you may think that you are developing all these skills and all this knowledge now. But research seems to be showing that most South African students are not well prepared for the job at all.

Recently *The Sunday Times* asked Graeme Addison (former University of North West professor) to set up a recruitment scheme for them. They wanted to find suitable young black journalists from around South Africa and prepare them for long-term careers in the newspaper. Addison visited most of the South African universities, technikons and commercial colleges that trained journalists and interviewed 117 candidates to be interns [journalists training on the job]. These candidates also wrote a two-hour test of language skills and news awareness.

Addison shares his findings in an article in the *Rhodes Journalism Review (Vol. 13)*. On the positive side, he says that students today have "an excellent grasp of the democratic role of media." He found that students were keen for newspapers to perform their watchdog role and expose misdeeds in places of power. But while he is thus impressed with the spirit and attitude of young future journalists, he has very disturbing things to say about their developing skills. His findings are as follows:

> *"Most journalism students don't:*
> - *know how to craft a narrative*
> - *know how to proofread copy*
> - *read newspapers*
> - *follow current affairs on the airwaves*
> - *read good books for pleasure*
> - *prepare for interviews*
> - *know about critical* [important] *developments in the media*
> - *know that they don't know"* [1]

Addison points out that many students have good computer skills nowadays. They can present material that looks attractive and many are skilled at finding information on the Internet. But he argues that *"high tech is no substitute for low cunning, a quality real journalists will always need."* [2] He found that students were poorly prepared to write stories that focus on issues rather than merely on facts. Yet print news needs journalists who can write searching stories that use many sources and look beyond the facts to interpret events [that is, evaluate events against their background, explore causes and possible results etc]. Journalists need to be able to explore issues in the areas of business, politics, education, labour, the environment and gender.

Addison says plainly that many institutions are not preparing young journalists very well for producing *"the issue-orientated news that is coming to fill much of the modern serious newspaper."* [3.]

As Addison himself is aware, the strong criticisms he makes in his article could provoke an angry reaction. It is hard for students and their institutions to consider that they may be less than the best. But students can use his observations to consider what action they can take and what skills they need to develop so that they can succeed in a very competitive field of work. He tells us quite plainly what *The Sunday Times* was looking for and what is in short supply amongst students.

In this book you can learn some of the basic craft of news writing. But it is also concerned with developing your power to reason, to interpret the events you cover as a journalist and to use different sources of news and information.

10 Minute Task

This task will help you to read the rest of the chapter with focus. Work with a partner if you prefer.

Take a newspaper, look through it carefully for a few minutes. Imagine that you are in charge of producing the next edition of the newspaper. Jot down some notes in response to the following questions. It does not matter if you still have little knowledge of newspapers; just try to judge and guess.
- *What steps would be needed to get all the stories in the newspaper to this point where it is printed and in a reader's hands?*
- *What different kinds of staff members would be needed and what would each kind do?*
- *What sections should the newspaper be divided into?*

Now read on and compare your own ideas with the information in the rest of the chapter.

The rest of this chapter will give you a brief overview of the new work-place you will enter as a journalist, the newspaper itself. We will look at the newsroom and the people who work there. You will follow the steps through which news moves as it develops from an idea in the news editor's mind into a printed story. Finally, we will describe the other departments which carry out the business functions of the newspaper.

Who does what in the newsroom?

General reporter: Most reporters start their careers as general reporters. This may change once their editor has evaluated their work. The general reporter normally starts the day without knowing where he/she will be or what they will be reporting about. The news editor will assign a story to the general reporter who will usu-ally cover local news. Often a general reporter gets assigned a story simply because there is nobody else to do it.

Beat reporter: The beat reporter works in a particular area or on a particular subject. A good example of a beat reporter is the court or crime reporter. A beat reporter has to know what is going on in their special beat. Mostly their stories will be about routine [everyday] events on their beat, but they must constantly search for unusual stories. A beat reporter has to try to *scoop* stories. *Scoop* means to get a major story ahead of your competitors. As a beat reporter you will be held responsible if, on the other hand, your competitors scoop you.

News editor: The news editor controls the news desk which is the heart of the newsroom. All news is gathered there. Editors of other sections like sports, business and entertainment all liaise [link up] with the news editor. The news editor supervises the general reporters.

Chief sub-editor: The chief sub-editor (usually just called *chief sub*) is in charge of the *copy desk*. The copy desk is where the pages of the newspaper are designed and the different stories are edited and arranged on the pages. Under the chief sub are the sub-editors (subs), who improve and polish stories. They must verify facts [that is, check whether facts are correct or not] and check the spelling of names and addresses. They also have to write headlines for all the stories. The chief sub enforces deadlines to ensure that the newspaper is produced on time.

Photographers: Photographers or photojournalists are very important because their photographs attract readers and involve them in the written story. They add drama, complexity and interest to the newspaper. The journalist and the photographer should be partners in journalism.

A photographer who is fully briefed [informed] on how the journalist wishes to tackle a story, will be alert to get the most fitting photo for that story. Photographers will find ways to actually improve the story through photographs. A story well illustrated with good photography is often chosen above a better story with no photographs.

Cartoonists: Most newspapers use cartoons to criticise and make fun of important people like government officials. Good cartoonists can sharply catch the mood and style of people and events in a drawing. They bring a special visual humour and interest to the newspaper.

Graphic illustrators: More and more newspapers are using drawings called graphics to make information clearer and livelier. Statistics about things like economic trends, the way taxes are divided or crime patterns often confuse readers. Graphics such as charts, bar graphs and line drawings can explain these things more clearly. The graphic illustrator has the job of choosing the most suitable graphic in each case. For example, charts can convey both written information and numbers.

Editor: The editor is responsible for the overall policy, strategic direction and management of the newspaper. The editor seldom gets involved in the newsroom or the day-to-day running of the news departments. The average reporter has little contact with the editor. The editor influences the work of the newspaper through the deputy editor and the assistant editors who report directly to the editor.

How does the newsroom work?

The newsroom is the heart of the news-gathering process. The newsroom is controlled by the news editor, who supervises this whole process. The news editor compiles a diary of jobs; briefs the reporters who will do them; monitors the day's or week's work (i.e. checks it while it is going on); checks the finished stories; liaises with the photographers and illustrators and answers queries. The news editor also keeps the editor and the chief sub-editor informed on how the work is progressing.

The newsroom has changed completely from what it was long ago. Journalists now sit at highly sophisticated computers rather than at typewriters. In South Africa most of the modern newspaper groups use Apple Macintosh computers and a publishing programme called QuarkXPress.

Even the atmosphere in the newsroom has changed. In the past, newsrooms were full of papers, talk and the endless chatter of type-writers. Computer technology has made the modern newsroom a far quieter place. A story can pass from the journalist to the news editor to the sub-editor and back to the journalist again without these three people having any personal contact and with little or no paper being used.

Now that laptop computers, modems and cellular telephones have appeared, the journalist does not have to be in the newsroom at all. For example, a sports journalist can take a laptop computer to a match and write the report while the match is in progress. When the match is over the reporter can immediately *download* [send the story by modem to the news editor]. This saves the newspaper and the journalist both time and money.

Technology has therefore made dramatic changes to the way things are done in the newsroom. But although reporters have moved to on-screen writing, their basic work of news gathering and reporting has not changed. This work is the main function of the newspaper itself and will not change even if newspapers become entirely elec-tronic.

Where do the stories covered in any one day come from? Many of them are diary stories that have been entered in advance into the newsroom diary and planned into that day's work. These stories would include major events, court cases, weddings, council meetings, etc. Although the events are known of before they happen, the real news comes from what actually happens at the event and what people say there.

Unexpected events also often occur and may be big news. When unexpected deaths, accidents, strikes, robberies, natural disasters and special political announcements take place, the news editor has to rearrange the day's coverage of expected events.

Tip-offs bring many stories too. [*Tip-offs are information from contacts about potential news*]. They often reach the newsroom by telephone. In fact, reporters do a lot of the day's news-gathering by telephone from the newsroom.

How does a story get from the reporter to the page?

A story starts with the reporter collecting all the facts, writing the story and then checking the story for accuracy. The reporter then passes the story to the news editor, who edits it and may suggest changes if necessary. The news editor then either returns the story to the reporter or sends it to the chief sub-editor.

The chief sub looks at the page layout plan and decides where the story will be placed in the newspaper. The chief sub then calculates how long the story must be and how big the headline must be. After this the chief sub passes it on to the sub-editor.

The sub-editor checks the story to ensure it is accurate and clear and is the correct size. If necessary, the sub-editor will also polish the writing to ensure that the story reads better. The sub-editor writes a suitable headline as well as a caption for any pictures or illustrations accompanying the story. The story then goes back to the chief sub for final checking.

Once the chief sub is satisfied that the whole page is complete and correct, the page is sent to production. The following diagram shows the way copy [the written stories] moves through the newsroom.

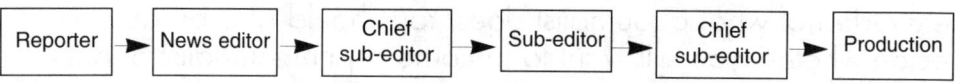

Other departments in the newspaper

A newspaper is a business and like other businesses has to make a profit for its shareholders. Several other departments carry out the business functions of the newspaper.

Administration: The administration department is responsible for important business functions of the newspaper. For example, it deals with salaries and wages, debtors and creditors, purchasing and also human resources.

Advertising: Most successful newspapers get most of their income from advertising sales, and most newspapers actually consist of up to 60 per cent advertising. Without advertising, very few newspapers could survive. Newspapers usually have two types of advertising: *display* and *classified.* Display advertisements are various sizes and are distributed throughout the newspaper, whereas the classified advertisements are small advertisements arranged in columns under different subjects in a special classified section of the newspaper.

Circulation: The circulation department has the job of distributing the newspaper, i.e. getting it into the hands of the readers. Copy sales come second to advertising sales in earning income for the newspaper.

Production: Production is the department where the newspaper is finally put together and printed.

Conclusion

Now that you have completed Chapter 1, you should have a much better idea of what a journalist does. You should also be able to decide whether you still want to become a print journalist or not. Good luck with your choice!

10 Minute Task

Now that you have read this chapter:
- *What things did you already know about journalism?*
- *Has anything you read been a big surprise to you?*
- *Has any aspect you read about been especially interesting for you?*
- *Have you changed your ideas about the way newspapers work or the kind of work you would like to do in journalism?*

Suggested Reading

1.   Addison, Graeme, Wasn't Eugene Nyati the one who fibbed about his CV at WITS, *Rhodes Journalism Review*, No 13, pp 34-35.

2.   Harris, Geoffrey, *Journalism Media Manual Practical Newspaper Reporting*, 2nd ed, Focal Press, 1993, pp 6-8, 26.

3.   Nel, Francois, *Writing for the Media*, Southern Book Publishers, 1994, pp 22-29.

4.   Teel, Leonard R, *et al*, *Into the Newsroom – An introduction to journalism*, Prentice-Hall, 1983, pp 69-83.

Ethics and the
2   Code of Conduct

Introduction

What did the title of this chapter mean to you? As you read it, did you ask: What are *ethics,* and why do I need to know about them? Actually, ethics are very important to journalists because they are the moral foundation for our work. In a way they are our guiding conscience.

People in all professions need to think about whether their work has a good effect or a bad effect on the lives of others. In journalism we must consider our readers and those whom we write about. We must try to benefit most people through our reporting and reach acceptable, responsible solutions. In guarding the public interest, we must avoid writing anything that causes people to commit crime or to take the law into their own hands.

Outcome

At the end of this chapter you should know the Code of Conduct for journalists and be able to apply the Code of Conduct when reporting. You should understand the various moral and ethical issues that are involved in reporting.

5 Minute Task

Before you read this chapter, use what you already know about newspapers and journalists to help you think of ways
- *journalists could harm others by their reporting;*
- *journalists could harm their own newspapers by their reporting;*
- *newspapers and journalists could prevent such harm being done.*

Note down your ideas on these points. Then read on to see how many of your ideas match ideas in the discussion.

Glossary of difficult words

It may help you to discuss the words below with a fellow student. Try to think of situations where they would be used. Then, as you come across them through the chapter, you will find them easier to understand.

professional	to do with one's main paid occupation
ethical	morally correct (behaviour)
distortion	a lie, a twisting of facts
suppression	preventing information from being seen, heard or known
disseminate	spread, broadcast, inform many people
conjecture	an idea/opinion based on little information or on wrong information
misrepresentation	lie, distortion, falsifying or disguising of information
prominence	fame, distinction, being seen by many
conscientious	dutiful, thorough and dedicated
intrusion	invasion, interruption that is unwanted
confidential source	information-giver who must be kept secret
plagiarism	copying, taking or presenting someone else's work as your own
attribute (to)	to take as coming from

Ethics: doing what is morally right

Ethics are the moral principles or the Code of Conduct which guide our behaviour. Journalists have to face ethical problems or dilemmas [difficult choices] daily and it is important that we have a Code of Conduct that we can refer to. According to Prof Guy Berger,

> "...journalism is not a neutral craft nor is it a technical skill. Choices confront journalists constantly, and decisions have to be made one way or another." [4.]

Since the early days of the press in South Africa the government has put pressure on journalists to make them report *responsibly*. Governments have even made laws to achieve this. As recently as 1996 President Mandela met with top black journalists to discuss the way they were reporting the ANCs performance with them.

But journalists usually resist when people outside the profession of journalism try to guide them about their journalistic ethics. In matters of conscience journalists prefer to be judged by their peers, i.e. by other journalists. The 9th principle of the International Federation of Journalists (IFJ) states:

> "Journalists worthy of that name shall deem it their duty to observe faithfully the principles stated above. Within the general law of each country the journalist shall recognise in professional matters the jurisdiction of colleagues only, to the exclusion of every kind of interference by governments or others." [5.]

The above does not mean that journalists are simply free to do and write what they like. As professionals they must work according to rules about what is news and what isn't news, as well as rules about how to write certain kinds of stories, and so on. Journalists are controlled by these journalistic traditions, by their employers and by their Code of Conduct itself. A journalist must follow the Code of Conduct or be prepared not to work as a journalist. But all journalists sometimes face situations where they do have to make an ethical choice. This decision may be a very difficult one.

If we as journalists see ourselves as the public's "watchdog" to guard against corruption and exploitation, we must make sure that our own morals and values are in order. We have to watch our own behaviour constantly. As one journalist says:

> "Journalism being what it is, even the most virtuous journalists, operating from what they see as the best of motives, inevitably will produce some morally unsatisfactory results. In either case it is worth understanding what went wrong and how to prevent its recurrence." [6.]

We will first consider some aspects of ethics and some ethical problems you could face as a journalist. Then we will look more closely at the Code of Conduct.

Libel

Journalists often face the threat of being charged with *libel.* What is libel? *Libel is any written or printed statement, or any sign, picture or effigy* [statue/figure made to represent a person], *not made in the public interest, tending to expose a person to public ridicule* [mockery, being laughed at as a fool] *or contempt or to injure his or her reputation in any way.*

Many journalists would say that you are not really a journalist if you have not been threatened with legal action for libel. This happens often because it can be hard to judge where a person's right to their reputation is more important than the public's right to know what is happening. A person's reputation is protected by law. A journalist can permanently damage someone's good standing in the community, sometimes without even intending to do so. If this damage is not done in the public interest it is called *defamation* and the newspaper can be *sued* [taken to court and charged].

Ethics: easier if we all saw the same thing

Journalism would be a lot easier (and very boring) if we all reported the same way. As everyone knows, all people were not born alike. Even people who speak the same language do not all understand things the same way. People have different beliefs, ideas and life experiences. They have many cultural differences. As a result, we simply do not all see the same event in the same manner.

If you have distrusted the police all your life, you can't easily understand why someone else does trust them. If you see a police-officer doing something, you will interpret their actions differently from someone who has grown up trusting the police. If you do not believe that the law protects you, you will not expect justice from the courts.

Two people seeing the same event will therefore report on it differently. If you compare the reports of different journalists who attended the same press conference you will find that their reports and even their quotes are different.

It is important that journalists learn to interpret the Code of Conduct as their peers would expect them to interpret it, because they must use good judgement in applying the Code of Conduct.

Ethics: what is the role of fairness?

Fairness is an essential part of healthy human relationships, because it basically means treating everyone equally and giving everyone an equal chance to be heard and understood. In journalism, the concept fairness means things like reporting *impartially* [not favouring any person or group over others], reporting completely so that aspects are not left out, and striving for balance so that different points of view come through. The Code of Conduct requires *fair* reporting.

During the liberation struggle in South Africa, the press was continually criticised by both the political left and the political right. Both sides strongly accused the press of unfair reporting during the State of Emergency in the 1980s. (Because of the restrictions placed on the press at this time, *The Star* newspaper suspended its Code of Conduct. The code was returned only when former State President De Klerk unbanned all the previously banned political parties, including the Communist Party.)

The issue of fairness can arise in different ways. For example, journalists need to be careful about the *amount* of information that they print. The amount of information we give a reader often depends on how much space is available on the page that day. As a result, readers may sometimes get so little information that they cannot judge whether a story has been reported fairly or not. It may be difficult for the journalist to change this situation.

Fair comment

What does the term *fair comment* mean? Some people offer their particular talent or service to the public for their judgement or approval. Politicians, public officials, entertainers and sports persons are typical examples of such people. Newspapers and other mass media have the right to comment on these people or criticise them. But the comment or criticism must be fair and without malice [wishing bad things on these people]. Also the comment should not deal with the private lives of the persons concerned. For example, it is fair comment to criticise public officials for their poor performance and point out that they lack ability or specialised knowledge, but it is not fair comment to reveal their sexual preferences.

Of course sometimes a reporter may serve the public best by reporting on a public person's private life. Then this would over-ride the usual rule.

NO ENTRY!

Mr Sleeze's bedroom - No entry to the press.

Striving for truth and accuracy

Journalists can talk about reporting the *truth*. But what is the truth? Philosophers have debated this question for centuries. For some people, truth is what they wish to hear and not what they need to hear or should hear. Identifying the truth is a big problem for journalists. James Retson of the *New York Times* is quoted as saying, *"You cannot merely report the literal truth. You have to explain it."* [7.] But, to explain the truth you still have to be able to identify it.

Is it impossible to be *objective* [unbiased, without personal prejudice] because we have difficulty in identifying the truth? A journalist can deal with this difficulty by interpreting events for the reader and giving as much background information to the news as possible. This doesn't mean that the journalist should mix news and opinion together.

Newspaper reports seldom get challenged for not being accurate or truthful. But readers have a right to truthful information and reporting, and being trustworthy to the reader is the basis of good journalism. It is therefore our fundamental duty to ensure that the news content is accurate and free from bias, and that all sides have been reported fairly.

Errors do happen when there is time pressure, as in newspaper publishing. We all do our best to avoid them, of course, but somehow the misspelt name or incorrect quote does slip through. Errors of fact and errors of omission [when things are left out] must be corrected in good time. Corrections should be published, even very prominently when necessary. If a paper or journalist makes too many mistakes they lose the respect and trust of the public. So it is important that you get your stories right the first time.

This is a high standard and impossible to maintain at all times. A shortage of time and space can limit the journalist's ability to report clearly and fully. There are other constraints too. For example, journalists must ensure that their reports will be understood by the *reasonable reader*, i.e. a reader who does not have specialised knowledge. Thus a journalist may have to cut complex and technical-sounding detail in a report, with the result that the report loses some fullness and complete accuracy. But at least the journalist must do his/her very best to achieve truth and accuracy.

Reporters must also use quotes from interviews in an ethical way. Only disreputable and dangerous reporters will deliberately alter or invent quotes to improve the impact of a story. They harm themselves, their readers and their newspaper when they do this. Both they and their newspaper will lose credibility [respect and trust] with their readers.

Sometimes a journalist who is trying to report truthfully and fairly may find that their newspaper does not give them the support they deserve. For example, a former student of mine came to see me one day to express extreme concern. He was covering [reporting on] the political violence of 1996 for a newspaper with strong ties to a political party based in KwaZulu-Natal.

His problem was as follows: After reading his story his editor insisted that the events that he had described and reported on could not have taken place. The editor then explained exactly what was supposed to have happened although the only information he had was what this young reporter had given him.

The Afrikaners have a wonderful expression: *Een oog is koning in die land van die blindes* (one eye is king in the land of the blind). The 'one-eyed' reporting that this editor was encouraging probably fed the flames of violence that ran through KwaZulu-Natal during the early 90s.

However, this very conscientious young reporter would not write something that he had not checked thoroughly. He was very concerned that his good name as a fair and accurate journalist was at risk. He has since moved on to another newspaper where he is allowed to do his job properly.

Impartiality: avoiding bias

Impartiality is part of fairness. It means to treat all sides in a dispute [argument, conflict] equally. However, it does not mean that the press must be unquestioning, or that journalists and editors cannot offer their opinions on a dispute. The important thing is to have a clear distinction between a news report and an opinion. Not only the writer but also the reader must be sure about what is a news report and what is an opinion: *Articles that contain opinion or the writer's personal interpretation should be clearly identified as doing so.* [8.]

The famous *CBS News* anchorman Walter Cronkite had this to say about reporting:

> *"I made every attempt to keep any hint of prejudice or bias, analysis or commentary, out of news reports....*
> *I believed that the straight presentation of news and a commentary by the same reporter would only confuse the public, although we in the profession know that it is possible for the same person to write a front page, factual, unbiased news report and a strong editorial on the same subject."* [9.]

To be *biased* means to unfairly prejudice someone or something. For the journalist it means losing accuracy and objectivity in reporting. A story becomes biased when the journalist's or editor's beliefs or values interfere with the reporting, and facts actually get distorted. If you believe that a particular group of people are better than another group, you may favour the one over the other in your writing.

For example, sports writers often show a distinct bias towards one team or another. As long as the public rely on the media to play a 'watchdog' role in society, unbiased reporting is obviously important.

 5 Minute Task

> *Do you agree with Walter Cronkite's statement on page 21? Can you keep all prejudice and bias out of a news report, or not? If not, why not? If possible, write down your response and explain it to a partner.*

Public trust

Because the newspaper is one of the most efficient forms of mass communication ever created, huge numbers of people read and trust newspapers. Journalists should guard this public trust in the press carefully. If trust is there, the press can play an important role in society: it can circulate information to enlighten and inform the public. In 1823 Thomas Jefferson wrote: *"The press is the best instrument for enlightening the mind of man, and improving him as a rational, moral, and social being."* [10.]

During the liberation struggle in South Africa, the alternative press played an important role of keeping the public informed about what was really happening. They paid a heavy price for doing so.

The press may not always earn approval for playing this role.

> *"The media need not ever be loved or even fully understood to carry out their function in society. But they must be trusted if they are to be credible in their watchdog role over the government, which has the power – with public backing – to restrict press freedom."* [11.]

It is important that the media report fully on what public figures are doing. This helps the public to decide whether these people are performing their duties properly or not. However the editor must finally decide what news will be made available to the public.

The editor must consider the question: *Do people need to know this?* or, *Is this information going to benefit our readers?* The public will trust the press if they feel that the press is working in the best interests of the public as a whole and not in the interests of any particular group. It is our duty to maintain the public trust at all times.

The press has the powerful ability to affect public opinion and persuade readers. It must not abuse this power. If the press lies to the public, even for a good reason (for example, to catch a criminal), the press betrays a trust and the public will never be sure whether they can trust what they read or not.

Freedom of the press

> *Freedom of the press belongs to the people. It must be defended against encroachment or assault from any quarter, public or private. Journalists must be constantly alert to see that the public's business is conducted in public. They must be vigilant against* [watch out for] *all who would exploit the public for selfish purposes.* [12.]

According to the *Code of Conduct of the South African Union of Journalists*, journalists have an obligation to defend the freedom of the press at all times. That obligation comes with the job, but it can lead to difficult decisions and painful consequences for the journalist.

Here is an example of such a situation. Recently, journalists were asked to leave a mass meeting at the University of Durban-Westville (UDW). The organisers of the meeting feared the negative and distorted publicity the university had been receiving in the press. I was one of the journalists at the meeting and I resisted leaving because I considered that the public had a right to know what happened there. Actually, the motion to exclude the press was proposed by a good friend of mine who usually strongly supports the idea of freedom of the press. He was misguided by his wish to protect the good name of the university. Fortunately, good sense won and I remained to do my job. By excluding me, the university would have made the public suspicious and would have further damaged its reputation as a free thinking, liberal institution. The public have a right to know and the public's business must be kept public.

There will always be attacks on press freedom by politicians who accuse journalists of being irresponsible. In 1996, President Mandela accused black journalists of not promoting the transformation of South African society. This is a serious charge from a person such as President Mandela, who met with senior black journalists in Cape Town to discuss the matter. The journalists listened to the President and noted his concerns. But they reminded him that the role of a free press is to inform the public of the true state of affairs. Then the public can decide for itself about the performance of government. Also, they pointed out, the press has to speak out when the rights and liberties of people are threatened. In other words, said these journalists, don't shoot the messenger. Both parties left the meeting with a better understanding of each other.

Influence and manipulation

People often accuse the press of abusing its power by manipulating public opinion. These accusations often come from government when the press point out defects [faults, weak parts] in proposed government policy. It is certainly true that the press has enormous influence and power with the public. And we must indeed ensure that we do not abuse that power.

But what do we mean by *manipulation*? You manipulate someone when you deliberately influence the choices that they make, but without actually forcing them to do what you want. You can also manipulate someone by altering the way they see their choices, i.e. their idea of what choices they could make. But you do this in such a way that you don't seem to be persuading them at all.

Manipulation is not always immoral in itself, but it can be done for immoral purposes. Therefore it requires explanation and justification. For example, the press itself may use manipulation in trying to influence smokers to give up the habit; but of course it can easily defend this 'good' kind of manipulation.

As you can imagine, manipulation is not used by the press alone. Business people, politicians and others may also wish to influence people's opinions and actions; and they constantly try to do this by manipulating the press itself.

Journalists can influence many kinds of events. A film critic can turn filmgoers against a particular film and therefore influence the box office takings for that film [i.e. the amount of money it makes]. Sports reporters can lobby [push] for the inclusion or exclusion of a certain player from a team. This manipulation may be based on reasons which are not objective. We may also draw people's attention to events that don't need or deserve such attention. So we can influence what happens, possibly in an unjustified or negative way.

Journalists should not fall into the trap of manipulating information improperly. In order to maintain public trust, journalists must be wary of manipulating and being manipulated.

Code of Conduct

The Code of Conduct and principles which follow, cover all the issues we have discussed in this chapter. Please consult the glossary on page 15 for explanations of words you find difficult. Also, if you find that one of the principles is worded in a way you find difficult, refer to that part of the chapter which discusses the principle you are struggling with.

The Code of Conduct of the South African Union of Journalists

1. A journalist has a duty to maintain the highest professional and ethical standards.

2. A journalist shall at all times defend the principle of freedom of the press and other media in relation to the collection of information and the expression of comment and criticism. He/she shall strive to eliminate distortion, news suppression and censorship.

3. A journalist shall strive to ensure that the information he/she disseminates is fair and accurate, avoid the expression of comment and conjecture as established fact and falsification by distortion, selection or misrepresentation.

---

4. A journalist shall rectify promptly any harmful inaccuracies, ensure that corrections and apologies receive due prominence and afford the right of reply to persons criticised when the issue is of sufficient importance.

5. A journalist shall obtain information, photographs and illustrations only by straightforward means. The use of other means can be justified only by the overriding considerations of the public interest. The journalist is entitled to exercise a personal conscientious objection to the use of such means.

6. Subject to justification by overriding consideration of public interest, a journalist shall do nothing which entails intrusion into private grief and distress.

7. A journalist shall protect confidential sources of information.

8. A journalist shall not accept bribes nor shall he/she allow other inducements to influence the performance of his/her professional duties.

9. A journalist shall not lend himself/herself to the distortion or the suppression of the truth because of advertising or other consideration.

10. A journalist shall not originate material which encourages discrimination on the grounds of race, colour, creed, gender or sexual orientation.

11. A journalist shall not take private advantage of information gained in the course of his/her duties before the information is public knowledge.

12. A journalist shall not engage in plagiarism and shall ascribe information used in articles to the original source or individual, organisation, media channel or news agency.

International Federation of Journalists: Principles on the Conduct of Journalists

1. Respect for truth and the right of the public to truth is the first duty of the journalist.

2. In pursuance of this duty, the journalist shall at all times defend the principles of freedom in the honest collection and publication of news, and of the right of fair comment and criticism.

3. The journalist shall report only in accordance with facts of which he/she knows the origin. The journalist shall not suppress essential information or falsify documents.

4. The journalist shall use only fair methods to obtain news, photographs and documents.

5. The journalist shall do the utmost to rectify any published information which is found to be harmfully inaccurate.

6. The journalist shall observe professional secrecy regarding the source of information obtained in confidence.

7. The journalist shall be aware of the danger of discrimination being furthered by the media, and shall do the utmost to avoid facilitating such discrimination based on, among other things, race, sex, sexual orientation, language, religion, political or other opinion, and national or social origins.

8. The journalist shall regard as grave professional offences the following: plagiarism; malicious misinterpretation; calumny, slander, libel, unfounded accusations; the acceptance of a bribe in any form in consideration of either publication or suppression.

9. Journalists worthy of that name shall deem it their duty to observe faithfully the principles stated above. Within the general law of each country the journalist shall recognise in professional matters the jurisdiction of colleagues only; to the exclusion of every kind of interference by governments or others.

Conclusion

Journalists face ethical and moral decisions daily and it is our duty to know and understand the Code of Conduct under which we work. We must, at all times, be keenly aware of the interests of society and our readers and ensure that our reporting does no harm. Journalists must refrain from actions that are not morally right. In so doing we maintain and strengthen our readers' trust in the press. Lastly, we must at all times defend the principle of freedom of the press. It is an obligation that comes with the job.

5 Minute Task

Now that you have read this chapter, consider:
- *What is the most important and basic ethical principle that should guide a journalist in all possible situations, in your opinion?*
- *Explain why you answer as you do.*
- *Discuss your answers in a group if possible, exchanging views freely.*

Suggested Reading

1. Hulteng, John L, *Playing it Straight*, The Globe Pequot Press, Connecticut, 1981, pp 44.

2. Klaidman, Stephen, *et al*, *The Virtuous Journalist*, New York, Oxford University Press, 1987, pp 5.

3. Nel, Francois, *Writing for the Media*, Southern Book Publishers, 1994, pp 197.

What is
3   news?

Introduction

The very simple question: *What is news?*, is probably the most important and difficult question in journalism. You will find out that there is no one single answer to this question. But it will affect your work as a journalist from day to day.

It is impossible for newspapers to report everything. Therefore we must know how to decide what is news and also what news is relevant to our own readers. We must be aware that what is news today will not be news tomorrow, news is always changing. Also, events are happening all the time but they are not news until someone tells someone else about them. News does not exist in isolation [by itself].

As you read further the idea of *news* will get easier to understand. Also, remember that news can change constantly but two important principles of news reporting will never change. *The need to report accurately and fairly remains the same.*

Outcome

At the end of this chapter you should understand what news is and what the traditional news tests are. You should know how to judge the value of news. You should be able to decide in each case whether the information that you have is news or not. You should know how to present news accurately, fairly and objectively. You should understand the importance of meeting your own readers' news wants, especially now that electronic media can deliver the news faster than newspapers can.

10 Minute Task

Before you read this chapter, think of any story that has recently been big news in a newspaper that you read. Then note down your ideas about why this story was news at all? As you read on, compare your ideas with the information in the rest of the chapter.

Defining news

Defining news is very difficult, and there is actually no universal definition of news, because news is a *relative* concept. This means that it is different from newspaper to newspaper, from place to place and from one time to another. You can test this statement by looking at any two local daily newspapers. You can be sure that the news carried on their front pages will not be exactly the same. Clearly, each news editor has a different view on what is the most important news for their readers' needs.

The following definitions show how difficult it is to define news:

News is anything published or broadcast.

News is an account of an event, or a fact or an opinion that interests people.

News is a presentation of a report on current events in a newspaper or other periodical or on radio and television. [13.]

News is anything that is timely that interests a number of readers, and the best news is that which has the greatest interest for the greatest number of people. [14.]

News is accurate and timely intelligence of happenings, discoveries, opinions and matters of any sort which affect or interest the readers. [15.]

News is everything that happens, the inspiration of happenings and the result of such happenings. [16.]

News comprises all current activities of general human interest, and the best news is that which interests the most readers. [17.]

Thus you can see that it is impossible to reach a satisfactory short description of news. However, there are two aspects of news that I consider especially important. Firstly, *news must be new,* i.e. new to those who hear it for the first time. Secondly, news is *"any printable story which in the opinion of the editor, will interest the readers of his paper* (or the audience of his broadcast)". [18.]

Traditional news tests

Editors have to sort through many ideas, events and *controversies* [arguments going on in society – usually about political or social issues] every day. They must decide which have real news value and they must also choose those which will actually be reported. Editors throughout the world use similar criteria to guide their decisions.

The basic factors that make news are as follows:

Timeliness: The news in a newspaper must be fresh: today's news is stale tomorrow and nobody wants stale news. Like vegetables, news is a perishable item and goes stale quickly.

These days, TV programmes like *CNN* and *Sky News* pick up events so quickly that newspapers must continually check the timeliness of their own news. In other words they must print the story of an event as soon after the event as possible. There is nothing more out of date than yesterday's newspaper.

Proximity/Relevance: People like to read news about people and events that are close to them. The closer an issue or an event is to your readers, the greater will be its impact and news value. Thus people are usually most interested in stories from their own city, province and country.

Community newspapers have grown in number although the local news that they contain would not get into the large daily or weekly newspapers. Community newspapers include news such as religious news, local school news and sports news. *"Readers want news to be relevant and to focus on them and where they live."* [19.]

Impact/Consequence: Any event or sequence of events that can affect a great number of people is obviously newsworthy. Therefore the number of people an event or idea affects, and also how seriously or dramatically it affects them, can tell us how important it is as news. Some events obviously have more consequence for readers than others have. News should be both dramatic and surprising, so that readers say, *"Wow! Have you heard this?"*

Journalists like to say that a dog biting a man is not news but a man biting a dog is. *Consequence* is a useful way to measure how newsworthy events such as floods, wars and political campaigns are. But we can't really use consequence to measure the newsworthiness of an event like a football match. Consequence is a good test of news about some kind of conflict, disaster or progress.

Prominence: As we all know, names make news: the bigger the name, the bigger the news. Not all readers are deeply interested in politicians, sports stars, singers and other personalities, but all readers do recognise names. Many readers are interested in what politicians, government officials and business leaders do and say, because it will affect their (the readers') own lives.

Of course, when people are regularly in the news, readers get interested in their behaviour. Although we should respect the privacy of prominent people, they must accept that their prominence makes the public curious about their daily lives.

Prominent people need the press to publicise what they say as much as the press need comments from them to make stories and sell newspapers. Some of these personalities feel that they must be seen with other prominent people. Notice the scramble by film stars, politicians, royalty and other pseudo [insincere, fake] personalities to rush to South Africa so that they can meet President Nelson Mandela and be seen with him, embracing him, if possible. Of course they hope that this will enhance their reputation and political correctness.

Novelty/Curiosity: People are insatiably interested in the unusual and the *bizarre* [odd, extraordinary]. The first or last or once-in-a-lifetime event is news. Once again: If a dog bites a man it is not news (because it is a common event), but a man biting a dog *is* news. Readers love to read about strange animals or striking animal behaviour, such as a dog that escapes from a kennel and walks 200 kilometres to find its owner. People like to read about things that are different, such as a new way to make a living, unusual habits and hobbies, and so on. To have novelty appeal, the reported item must be unusual and provoke people's curiosity. Although most people like to deny it, they are attracted to articles on sex, perversion [abnormal or unnatural behaviour], psychic phenomena [things that can't be explained by science] and violence.

> "While most professional journalists today will agree that serious newspapers should avoid sensationalism, such stories do make news. The generally conservative Charles Dana's own creed at the New York Sun was: "I have always felt that whatever the Divine Providence permitted to occur I was not too proud to report." [20.]

Conflict: A quick check through our daily newspapers and TV and radio broadcasts will show you that war, political issues and crime (followed very closely by sport) are the most common news of all. Even when these news items are not directly about war, it is the conflict in them that makes them newsworthy. People love to read about politicians attacking each other in the press; differences of ideology make news. Most conflicts are newsworthy, and physical conflict is especially newsworthy because injury and damage often results. Violence usually makes news because of the emotions it arouses.

A fight between two footballers in a match might not get much attention from the editor, but a violent clash between two groups of opposing fans could get front page coverage. Also, conflict naturally leads to tension and suspense which have news value in themselves.

Does the printing of stories depicting [describing] violence lead to more acts of violence, or not? Will the perpetrators [doers] of violence continue with their activities because they are sure to get publicity this way? I would say *no*, this argument isn't valid. However, there is much debate about these points and many who feel that we should be very *circumspect* [cautious, reserved] with our reporting of violence.

Human interest: Many stories that appear in our press don't really satisfy any of the above news tests. These stories usually fit into the category of *human interest*. For example, people love stories about children and animals. Newspapers often use pictures of animals and children to promote various causes. People love to read about people, and today many editors look for a human interest angle in almost all stories – that is, they should have human interest as well as other news value. Although human interest is not strictly a news value measurement, it has important story value. It enriches the news by getting readers to identify with [feel for] people they read about. Some stories even get rejected because they have little human interest angle. Sometimes journalists have to look closely at the situation and events in a story before they can decide whether to treat it as a human interest story or as a straight news item.

Sex: As much as some people would like to deny it, sex has great news value. People like to follow the personal lives of the rich and famous. Take for instance the enormous interest that the public showed in the divorce proceedings of Nelson and Winnie Mandela. This interest is continued in the worldwide public interest in members of the British royal family. The South African public is also fascinated by the relationship between President Mandela and Graca Machel of Mozambique. In the above examples, prominence links up with sex as a news value. Sometimes sex links more with novelty, e.g. the unusual sexual practices of a person who is otherwise unknown.

Simple interest and enjoyment: People sometimes want to sit down and relax with a newspaper. At such times, hard news may depress or stress them; but they will still remain hooked on the paper if they simply enjoy reading it.

A paper that people buy mainly for the essential information it carries may easily become dull if it does not have enjoyable, easy-to-read articles. These might have human interest or any other news values discussed above but they might also appeal to particular interests such as education, self-help, entertainment, cultural ritual, travel – or just interesting *trivia* [small, unimportant items]. The interest and enjoyment such stories offer is a news value in itself.

Let's consider the importance of *humour*. Cartoons are so popular because people demand a lighter side to the news. People want to laugh. They love trivia and without trivia, newspapers would be very boring.

Assessing news value

Now that you have looked at some news values, we can move on and consider how you will apply this knowledge quickly and efficiently when you are at work.

What do readers want most from their newspapers? Which news value should a reporter always bear in mind? Well, the first thing readers want is news which is *relevant to them*. Readers want news which relates to them and to the place where they live; but, on the other hand, they do not want their newspaper to ignore relevant events in other parts of the world.

Readers don't especially want a newspaper that just *looks* attractive. The heart of a newspaper is its news content and that must be good. You cannot fool readers with fancy design and layout, if there is little solid news in the newspaper. Also, if the design and layout style does nothing to enhance the news and make the newspaper easier to read, it is not worth using.

As well as hard news, an important thing that readers want from newspapers is tips and advice on how to improve their lifestyles. So let's focus on what qualities news must have?

1. *News must be new.*

2. *News must have conversational value.* If we don't want to talk about it, it has no news value. The conversational value comes from all the criteria we have been discussing so far: relevance, prominence, consequence, human interest, novelty, etc.

3. *News must have commercial value.* This of course relates to 1. and 2. If our readers are not interested in the news that we bring to them they will soon stop buying our news-paper. News, like most things, is a commodity that can be bought and sold. This is very important and we should consider it more closely.

Remember that you can decide news value by using a simple, basic measure: *what readers want.* This can be different in different times and places and it is risky to ignore what readers want when you are deciding what is news. For example, at the start of the Truth and Reconciliation Commission (TRC), *The Cape Times* dedicated a number of pages and appointed a number of journalists to cover this important and historic event. But the immediate result was a drop in circulation. The general reader of this newspaper was not interested in the amount of news about the TRC that they were getting so they showed their frustration by not buying the paper.

Another example of this pattern was the history of *The Rand Daily Mail*, one of South Africa's best newspapers. The editorial policy showed great dedication to informing the public about the state of the country and the extent of human rights abuse in South Africa. But the newspaper's reading public was not ready to accept the information. Consequently, the newspaper lost advertisers and readership and was forced to close down.

The accurate assessment of our readers' news wants is essential if we wish to remain in business. Many students believe that news-papers should only give readers the facts and what they need to know to make accurate assessments of the situation. While we can admire this attitude, it may not be enough to keep a newspaper in business. A newspaper is a business and needs to sell advertising and copy to survive. As in other businesses, the customer comes first. People buy newspapers for different reasons, e.g. for the advertising, the news, the leisure and entertainment or for the sport.

How do we decide on the *importance* of any item of news? Well, firstly we should measure a news item on how important it is to the readers compared with other news stories which could compete with this item for the same space. Next we should consider its real or intrinsic importance, so that we can decide how much space it should get. Here we have to be as objective as we can (this is discussed below). Finally we should not neglect another important measurement, journalist's *intuition* [the power of understanding something quickly, without reasoning it out].

Here are some aspects you can use to measure a story's importance.

1. How much disruption was caused to everyday life?
2. How many people were affected?

3.   How close was the event to the readers?
4.   How long ago did the event take place?
5.   What was the outcome or result of the event?

Lastly, it is important to bear in mind the mix or variety of our traditional news tests. A car hijacking is not usually very big news. However, the first car hijacking which has occurred in a quiet small town is big news for the people in that district. And the hijacking of the car of a prominent politician is big news generally. It is even bigger news if it took place outside a police station in full view of high ranking police officers who took no action because they were off duty and do not receive danger pay when not on duty.

10 Minute Task

Work with a partner or group if possible. Look at the front page of any newspaper that is at hand. Re-assess the news value of the stories on the page.
• Do you agree that all the front page stories have front page news value?
• What kinds of news value does each have, in your view?
• If you were in charge, would you have put these stories in the same order of importance? Would you have swopped the lead story for another on that page or even from an inside page? If so, why?

Presenting news objectively, fairly and accurately

So far, we have discussed how the journalist judges what is news and what isn't. But, news is not only something 'out there' that the reporter looks for. News is also something that reporters *process* [develop, work on] as they research and write a news story. When readers talk about the news in the newspaper they are talking about the news that the reporter has already discovered, selected and presented as a news story. Important questions arise about this *prepared* 'news'. Whose idea of news are we reading? And how accurate is this news? Are we seeing all sides of the picture? Can we trust that it is true? These issues have been raised already in Chapter 2. Now you will deepen your understanding of them so that you can apply this understanding when you are deciding how newsworthy a story is and how you should present this news.

Let me tell you what happened. No listen to me.

Objectivity and subjectivity

One of the most common accusations that journalists face is the accusation that they are not *objective*. But what is it to be objective? Objective means *detached, fair, impersonal, impartial, unbiased and unprejudiced.* Subjective on the other hand means *based on personal bias.*

In modern journalism, objectivity is our ideal. But can we achieve true objectivity? The history of the press shows that early newspapers were certainly not objective and were filled with opinion, with biting sarcasm and with personal bias. It is clear that journalists started to search for objectivity only more recently. However, it is also clear that we don't all see the same event through the same eyes. Thus objectivity in journalism must be difficult or even impossible to achieve.

Have you ever watched a televised boxing match? If you watch the fight closely you will sometimes notice that the commentary you hear does not seem to match the fight you are watching. The reason is quite simple. The TV commentators are based at ringside which is below ring level, so that the commentators have to look up at the fight. But the TV cameras are usually positioned high up around the ring looking down at the fight. The commentators are commenting on what they are seeing, but because of their positioning, they are not able to see all the action. As we watch TV we see what the TV camera operators see, but this may not be what the commentators are seeing. There are different views of the same event. You can see how the commentators and the camera operators could make very different decisions about what parts or aspects of the fight they should emphasise, i.e. what has news value.

Not only do we see events from different angles, we also bring a lifetime of personal experience to every event we witness. No matter how objective we try to be, those life experiences will interfere with our way of seeing things. Subjectivity is sure to enter into our reporting. *Why?* you may ask, "*I reported exactly what I saw happen.*" In fact that is exactly the problem. Usually *the reporter is the observer, interpreter, writer, and judge of what information goes into each story.* But it is important that we try very hard to be impartial [fair, unbiased] when assessing and reporting news. A reporter must consider news value from all angles, and a story must pass through checks and balances before it is printed. All stories must be checked carefully by experienced editors. Your editor will expect you to report without personal bias because s/he knows that is what readers demand.

Accuracy and fairness

In addition, in seeking news we must look for the truth or at least, as Bob Woodward expressed it, "*the best possible version of the truth.*" [21.] As we discussed in Chapter 2, newspaper reports very seldom get challenged, but that does not give journalists the right to publish information that is not accurate or truthful. The reporter's idea of news value should never get in the way of the facts. Readers have a right to truthful information and reporting and as we have already pointed out, good faith with the reader is basic to good journalism. Our first duty is then to ensure that *the news content is accurate and free from bias and that all sides have been reported fairly.*

Although it is the reporter's job to find and write the facts, the task is not that easy. How does a journalist know when they have achieved the *best possible version of the truth?* The only answer is that if we are satisfied that our story is accurate and fair, then we have achieved as much as is possible.

Accuracy is the most important aspect of any story. No matter how newsworthy an event is, if you report it inaccurately your story will not be proper news. Get the facts straight and the rest will usually look after itself. Here are some essential guidelines on accuracy for every reporter:

1. *The spelling of all names must be correct.* A misspelt name can and often does lead to embarrassment and possible legal action against the newspaper.
2. *Every quote must be exactly what was said* and *how* it was said.
3. *Numbers must add up.*
4. *Dates and times must be accurate.*

But even if you have done all this, it is still not good enough. Even if your details are correct you can still mislead the reader if the details are not placed clearly *in context,* i.e. so that the surrounding events and circumstances are clear. To obtain the best version of the truth your reporting must be accurate and in context. However, that still does not imply that your story is fair.

What do we mean by being fair? Accuracy and fairness are related but they are not the same. Think of it like this: *"As reporters we act as the eyes and ears of our readers, with the power to give them information – or to hold it back"* [22.] How we present a story is how the reader will receive it and react to it. Thus, if we want the public to trust us they must be able to see that we are providing accurate information on all sides or aspects of an issue.

Reporters often have to cover controversial situations in which there are major conflicts of values. There is seldom only one viewpoint in a story and in political stories there will be many viewpoints from opposing sides. For the sake of fairness, *everyone involved in the story must get the opportunity to respond.* This is especially important for those in the story whose integrity or competence is being questioned. We must remove our own biases from the story.

The more we strive for fairness and objectivity in our stories the more balanced our stories will become. To be balanced, the reporter must let all contrasting points of view be represented. That does not mean that you have to quote everybody, but it means that you must at least acknowledge different points of view. Here are a few rules that you should apply to ensure that your story is fair and balanced:

1. *Stick to the facts* – never manufacture facts.
2. *Do not give your own opinion.* If you do, you will be seen as biased.
3. *Listen to the advice of your editor* – the editor has been there many times before.
4. *Go easy with your choice of adjectives* – just tell the story.
5. Remember *you are an observer* and a *reporter, not a player* in the story.
6. Do not get too close to the story.
7. *If someone has something relevant to say, give him/her a forum.*
8. *Remember that your story could ruin a person's good name.*

Changing perspectives

One of the modern newspaper's big problems is the fact that other news sources can deliver the news long before newspapers can. Television and radio can get news to us almost immediately, *CNN* is a good example of this. However, a newspaper is normally up to eight hours behind in its delivery of news. Less than 30 minutes after the horrific Oklahoma bomb blast, a TV station had set up a mobile studio at the scene and had begun to broadcast to the USA and the rest of the world. How can newspapers compete with that speed? Obviously, most of their stories will be a rehash of what has been broadcast.

Because newspapers can never compete with the electronic media for speed of delivery, they must instead try to be more *innovative* [inventive, full of new ideas]. Instead of rehashing what has already been broadcast, newspapers must look at the news in more depth, seeking a different *angle* or *perspective*.

In the case of the Oklahoma bomb blast, newspapers set up teams of journalists to look for different angles. The first papers to report tried to link the blast to Muslim extremists and the later papers, look-ing for their own *niche* [angle, approach], tried to link the blast to local religious extremists.

Journalists must try to deliver information that is valuable and difficult for the opposition to copy. Readers must want to buy *your* news-paper; so your presentation of the news must go beyond what was on *CNN* or *SATV* news.

Generally, newspapers will have to move closer to their readers. They will need to ask very seriously, *What do the readers want to read about? What are the hopes and aspirations of the average reader?* Newspapers should voice the concerns of their readers and hold politicians and bureaucrats responsible where necessary. Finally, editors and journalists should never forget that their readers are vital to the survival of the newspaper. Newspapers should continually research the wants and interests of their readers.

Unfortunately, hardly any newspapers do true, effective market research. Most newspapers will probably disagree with me when I say that they usually conduct research only to confirm their own existing ideas and not to find out the real situation. For example, a local newspaper uses a focus group of four Indian families to research their news presentation to an Indian population of almost one million.

If you want to know what people want, ask them! People's interests tend to change, so we must keep re-evaluating our methods of presentation.

10 Minute Task

> Read through any news story in a newspaper that is available. Is the story accurate, fair and as balanced and objective as possible? Explain the reasons for your assessment. Share your notes with your partner/group/class.

Conclusion

In this chapter you have learnt that in order to report effectively, it is essential that you understand what news is and how to assess the news value of a story. You should now be able to assess your readers' news wants. You should understand that this is important because news is a tradeable commodity and your newspaper needs to survive as a business. Lastly, you have learnt the importance of ensuring that your reporting is accurate, fair and objective.

Suggested Reading

1. Berry, Thomas Elliot, *Journalism in America*, New York, Hasting House Publishers, 1976.

2. Brooks, Brian S, *et al*, The Missouri Group, *News Reporting & Writing*, New York, St Martins Press, 4th edition, 1992.

3. Harriss, Julian, *et al*, *The Complete Reporter*, New York, MacMillan Publishing, 4th edition, 1981.

4. Nel, Francois, *Writing for the Media*, Southern Book Publishers, 1994.

5. Teel, Leonard R, *et al*, *Into the Newsroom – An introduction to journalism*, Prentice-Hall, 1983.

6. Ward, Hiley H, *Professional Newswriting*, New York, Harcourt Brace Jovanovich, Publishers, 1985.

Sources of
4   news

 Introduction

People have a deep need for news. They not only need it, they generally demand it. You can see this clearly in people who have been cut off from the outside world for some time. When they return to normal life, they immediately start to catch up on the news in their families, their local communities and the world.

When we meet friends we ask, *How are you, what have you been doing?* This shows our inborn thirst for news. A reporter responds to this thirst by seeking out the news, evaluating whether it is sound and accurate and bringing it to readers.

 Outcome

At the end of this chapter, you will understand where news comes from, what the traditional news sources are, and how to evaluate news sources and their motives. Finally, you will be able to start developing your own contacts for news.

The reporter with a 'nose'

The ability of the reporter is the most important factor in news-gathering. Old journalists describe this ability as having a *nose for news*. Not all reporters have this 'nose' for a story and those who don't have it must build their skill at news-gathering. They must develop as many contacts as possible who will feed them with sources of news and stories.

Stories generally come from *outside* the newspaper. One study found that approximately 49 out of 50 ideas used in the paper on a particular day came from outside; only one came from the staff. Therefore, editors want reporters who go out daily to find new stories and come up with creative ideas. They know that good quality news and creative reporting will put their paper ahead of the others with readers.

5 Minute Task

> • *Look at the next heading, but don't read any further than that.*
> • *Now 'brainstorm' a list of all the things you could do in order to get ideas for stories. Work quickly, don't throw any ideas out and don't try to order your ideas.*
> • *Now read on and see if your ideas match ours or not.*

Finding the story: How do you generate ideas?

Most story ideas are the result of a greedy curiosity, an active imagination, and help from fellow journalists. Even the most dedicated and creative journalists run out of ideas now and then. So, we must have a source of ideas that work for any time or place, and especially when the usual well of ideas dries up for a while.

When my students attend their first lecture, I tell them that to be good journalists they will need the following items most of all: big ears to listen, good eyes to observe, a good nose to sniff out a story, curiosity about everything and a burning desire to tell everybody what they have just found out. Obviously, there is more to reporting than these things, but they certainly give a good start.

Here are a few ideas on how to generate ideas for stories:

Read: Read, read, read, read. The sad truth is that today's students do not read – not even for pleasure – although reading is the lifeblood of all journalists. As a journalist you should read everything that you can put your hands on, including all the opposition newspapers, brochures and magazines. Study the work of the most popular journalists. You can learn from the topics and content they use, as well as the approach to the story and the style. You can even copy their ideas and their style of writing, but not their exact words; these have copyright. You can take good ideas that you find and adapt them for local conditions and for your own readers.

Listen: This is the most important skill you can develop. Many journalists become boring because they spend too much time talking about their own exploits [experiences and achievements] instead of listening and focusing on others. If you listen rather than speak you can learn much; and you may well hear something interesting that sparks an idea for a future story. Listening is not just passive 'hearing', it is an active, productive talent which can bring you much information.

Circulate: Get around town – go out and meet people. Every month, try to attend an event that you would not normally attend. Meet people out of their work environment when they are relaxed. Listen to their conversations. Find out what interests people, what excites them, what angers them. These people are your readers and there is no better source of ideas than them.

Be friendly: Someone once said, *"Be nice to people, not because you might meet them on the way down, but because it is a damn nice way to do business."* If you consider yourself better than other people, your arrogance will be your downfall. People are key to your success as a journalist and they can also lead to your failure. The best journalists make friends with beggars, street vendors, bartenders, clerks, hotel receptionists, tea makers, police, paramedics, petty criminals, that is, with almost everybody.

Identify and meet leaders: Make the effort to identify and get to know *key people* [people who have knowledge, responsibility, power]. Take them to lunch or plan to meet them at social occasions, meetings and clubs. It is easier to interview key people if they know who you are before the interview. You may never need to interview these key people but you should at least establish them as contacts who may introduce you to other key people. The trust of key people is essential, for a good journalist. Never break your word to them, as this will undo all your good work.

Visit your library: Browse through the notice boards at your local library. They will tell you a lot about what is happening in the community. Be alert to local interest.

Read records: Government departments are full of records. Seek out these records and scan them to find out about employment, property sales, financial dealings, new businesses and bankruptcies and indeed all the activities of businesses and individuals that will lead to a good story. Get to know the people who keep and work with the files because they can give you leads to interesting information.

Subscribe: Get on as many mailing lists as you can. The *'junk'* in your mail box might be the source of your next story.

Be sceptical: Good reporters are always *sceptical.* In other words, they suspect that the truth is not quite as it appears. For example, you may hear a story about the charity work of a community leader. But if you speak to the leader's employees, friends and family, you may get a totally different picture. Most people have a dark side to their character, and in this kind of story, further investigation may reveal it. *Always be aware that the truth may be quite different or even completely opposite to the first picture you get.* By checking the facts you may find an alternative story. Even better: you may land an exclusive story.

Become an expert: The more you know about a particular subject, the better prepared you will be when you want to probe [investigate] deeper. You can develop expertise in any subject by reading about experts in that subject, and/or asking them questions. If you can't meet the expert face to face, develop the habit of asking questions as you read. In short, ask as many questions as possible. In this way your knowledge will grow: the more you know about the subject the better you will be able to ask more and more probing questions about that subject.

Check through advertisements: Advertisements, particularly the classifieds, are often a source of interesting stories. You may find someone trying to sell stolen goods or you could find a disgruntled wife selling her adulterous husband's BMW motorcar for R5.

Study community newspapers: Community news can be a rich source of stories. Most of the stories have not caught the attention of the mainstream press, but they may be full of possibilities.

Question yourself, consult yourself: Basically, it is you who must be alert to look and listen to what is going on around you. Ask yourself: *Why do people behave the way they do? What are they thinking about? What are the fears and anxieties of the people in this situation?* Always ask yourself the most important question: *why?* and then look for the answer. Journalists who attune themselves to people will find a rich source of human interest stories right on their own doorsteps.

Developing your own sources

We have now looked at different ways in which you could get ideas for stories. Perhaps you have already noticed that finding ideas will usually connect you with *people* who provide information in one way or another. And as you begin your career as a journalist you will soon start to meet interesting people in various walks of life. As you meet more and more people you should always be alert to find people who are influential and knowledgeable about what is going on in their community, organisation or business. Most of the information used in stories comes from a reporter's personal sources – people. Journalists usually divide these personal sources into three groups: *contacts, tipsters* and *informants*.

A *contact* is usually someone who everyone recognises as the person with information on a specific subject. For example, a company's public relations officer can be considered a contact and may be referred to (in a story) as a spokesperson.

A *tipster* may have information or may only point to a source of information. A tipster's information is usually unsubstantiated. This means that it is information that is not yet proven or certainly true. Tipsters are usually *anonymous* [they don't give their name or they don't want others to know it]. Their information gives the reporter a start on a story. The reporter is able to question the authorities and seek an explanation for what the tipster hinted at or suggested. *Informants* are often referred to as *leaks*. I will discuss leaks later in the chapter.

 10 Minute Task

> Before you read on, respond to these questions:
> • What kind of people would you look for as sources?
> • How would you keep your sources going over a long time?
> • How would you know which sources are really useful and
>   which are not?
> Now read on and compare your ideas with what follows.

How can you develop your own personal sources?

Develop your own contact book: As you meet influential and knowledgeable people, write down their names and contact details in a contact book that you can refer to when you need to speak to them. You can use a directory, notebook or file cards for this purpose. Your contact book will be your most prized possession as you continue with your career as a journalist. A good contact book takes many years to develop and is something that a journalist will never lend. The contacts that you develop are your eyes and ears and therefore a valuable asset. Why not keep a duplicate contact book safely somewhere, in case the original gets lost or stolen? Also, you may need to be particularly careful with the details of sources who insist on *confidentiality* (i.e. those who refuse to be named or revealed). If you prefer, you could keep their names and addresses in a separate place.

From time to time you should review the names in your contact book to refresh your memory about the people you have met. If you have not spoken to your contacts for some time, it is a good idea to telephone them, just to ask them how things are going and say you are still there.

Visit the scene: Always visit the scene of your story. First hand knowledge is basic to good reporting. This means that even when you are not chasing a particular story, you need to be building

Tom Xulu reporting from the scene.

contacts on your beat. Visit all the departments or organisations on your beat and find a person in each who is willing to talk to the press. Attend as many of the functions, meetings and seminars on your beat as you can. Make a note of those people who seem friendly and positive towards you. Then, when a story comes up you will have a good knowledge of the background context and the contacts you could use.

Remember the 'little' people: Secretaries may not seem to be important people, but they are excellent sources of information. They have access to people and usually know what is happening in their organisation. Secretaries can be most helpful in tracking down their bosses or the important information you need just before deadline. Don't forget the 'faceless' people in an organisation – the support staff who are not as visible as the 'professional' staff. Who are they? The tea person, security guards, drivers, clerks and messengers. These people are often very aware of what is going on in an organisation but because they are not seen as important, they are ignored. Show them that you consider them important and you may have a valuable source of information. Your big story may come from these people.

Meet influential people: Meet as many of the influential people on your beat as you can. Get to know them and (more important) get them to know you. If you can, take them out to lunch.

Protect your sources: This is not just good advice. If you look back at Chapter 2 you will recall that the journalist's code of ethics actually *demands* it. The International Federation of Journalists' *Principles on the Conduct of Journalists* says: *The journalist shall observe professional secrecy regarding the source of information obtained in confidence.* The Code of Conduct of the South African Union of Journalists says: *A journalist shall protect confidential sources of information.* Journalists have been jailed for not revealing their sources, and most journalists would be reluctant to work with another journalist who did not respect the confidentiality of a source. You must be careful not to write anything that could harm your source, your newspaper or yourself. Many people have lost their jobs because they have spoken to the press.

Check the telephone directory: The telephone directory is helpful
not only for finding people but also for verifying names and
addresses. Get to know the layout of the telephone directory and
save yourself valuable time. It is a good idea to study your area
telephone directory in detail so that you know how the numbers
have been classified. For instance, are schools listed together or are
they distributed through the directory according to their names?
What about government and quasi-government organisations?

Evaluating sources

You may think that it is always the reporter who must find his/her
sources of news. The real situation is more complex. In this section,
we will look at sources, who approach the press themselves. Herbert
J Gans said in his book, *Deciding What's News*:

> *"The relationship between sources and journalists resem-*
> *bles a dance; for sources seek access to journalists and*
> *journalists seek access to sources. Although it takes two to*
> *tango... more often than not, sources do the leading."* [23.]

Journalists need to have ways of deciding whether sources are reliable and worthwhile or not. This is not easy, because the motives of
sources are not always clear. Some sources are clearly self-serving,
politicians often fit this type. But the motives of other sources may
seem quite unselfish, or they may be self-serving in a rather complex
way. Sources can be concerned citizens, dissatisfied employees or
people looking for revenge. You will probably agree that the motives
of sources like these are probably not one simple motive. For this
reason we will examine the various types of sources and leaks and
explain the special vocabulary associated with leaks.

A *true leak* happens when a source offers information that the
journalist generally has not asked for. The information is given on
condition that the leaker remains anonymous.

Often governments leak information deliberately to the press to find
out how the public will respond to a new policy or proposed action.
Journalists call this deliberate, authorised leak *a plant.* A government
uses plants to promote its administration and its interest.

Leaks occur most in times of crisis. Although sources have various motives for leaking information (we will discuss these later), they do usually have one purpose in common: that is, *to serve their own vested interests*. Remaining anonymous protects the source because although the journalist gets a story ahead of competitors, the source can deny after publication that he/she gave any information to the journalist.

But why do people leak information to the press? It is important to find out what the source wants. There are widely different motives:

The Ego leak: Here the source wishes to satisfy a sense of his/her own importance. This is probably the most common form of leak, but the leaks are usually not major ones. Few people do something for nothing. Sources generally supply information with a return in mind. For a charitable source, this return could be something like the benefit of society.

The Goodwill leak: Here the source wishes to earn favour with the journalist and probably expects the the journalist to return the favour at a later date. Some sources may feel they need the journalist as an ally and may appear to give information freely without selfish motives.

The Animus leak: This type of leak is used mainly by politicians. Its main purpose is to embarrass another person or party.

The Policy leak: This is where documents or inside information are used to get attention from the press so that a policy can be either promoted or attacked. The issue might not really be worth much attention without the inside information that is leaked.

The Trial Balloon leak: In this case, a controversial policy which is still being considered gets 'leaked' in order to test public opinion before it is officially released. If there is an unfavourable public reaction to the policy it can be modified before it is made official.

The Whistle-blower: This type of leak is different from the others. It usually happens when a civil servant feels that he/she cannot right a wrong through the usual and 'proper' channels. In this case, the leaker is often willing to state his/her case in public, and be named. Such leakers may even risk losing their jobs.

In dealing with the press, officials often protect themselves by demanding how journalists should describe the way the information came to them. They may say the information is either *on the record* or *off the record.*

On the record: This means that all statements are directly quotable, by name and title, to the person who is making the statement.

Off the record: Information given off the record is for the journalist's knowledge only and is not to be printed or made public in any way. The information also cannot be taken to another source to obtain official confirmation. The source usually provides off-the-record information in order to prevent the journalist speculating incorrectly.

Basic research

One of the basic rules of journalism is that the more information you uncover, the sounder your judgements will be and the more accurate your story will be, too. No matter how skilled a writer you are, if you lack information your story will not have a solid foundation. On the other hand, *good* reporting is frequently backed by obvious good research. Research can equip the journalist not only to report on what is happening but also to give background information and perspective to a story.

Some journalists argue that too much research spoils a good story because it makes you lose focus. Others believe that too much research prevents reporters from meeting their deadlines. There are no easy answers to these accusations, journalists do have to learn to research economically. However, I propose that they should do so, because there can be no substitute for good research.

In this section we will look at two resources the modern journalist should use routinely when researching stories, official records and the computer.

Using official records

Interactions between people are recorded in many different ways. We go through life leaving a trail of recorded information that is easily accessible to researchers. Although at first these records may not look very interesting, reporters can use them to obtain fascinating evidence about what people do. Most records are open to public scrutiny [i.e. anyone may look at them]. Here are some public records you may wish to examine.

Police and court records: Does a person have a criminal record? How many convictions a person has – and what they are for – can lead to an interesting story.

Birth records: If you suspect a person is lying about his/her age and correct name, checking the person's birth certificate can set the record straight. You can also identify who the parents are and the place of birth.

Death records: A death certificate will provide evidence of the time, place and cause of death.

Property register: All land ownership is registered at the Deeds Office. You will be able to determine the ownership and previous ownership, back to the first owner of the land.

Judgements: These records can help to reveal a person's credit standing.

Other records that you may wish to examine include voter registrations or voters' rolls, permits and inspection reports and marriage and divorce records. Not only do these records provide useful information but they also ensure that the information you report is accurate.

You may have to pay a search fee to access records, or you may have to request permission in advance from the relevant authority before examining certain records. Check first with the relevant authority for the correct search *protocol* [procedure]. *But never state the reason why you wish to examine the records, this is not their business.*

Computer-assisted reporting

All newspapers today are equipped with computers that are connected to e-mail and the Internet. How does this affect journalists researching stories?

Firstly, the Internet has made enormous quantities of information available. It is an advanced tool for learning and research which gives you access to databases worldwide. Wherever you are on the planet you can connect with the best libraries and universities in the world.

You can also have access to most of the foremost newspapers in the world (which are nearly all online), as well as news services such as *Reuters* and *Associated Press*. The Internet has databases with up-to-date information on almost every subject you can imagine.

Secondly, you can share ideas and network with others as you gather information. Internet and the e-mail puts you immediately and cheaply in contact with people and other journalists around the world. As a local journalist you can become familiar with media issues both here and abroad.

Thirdly, one of the most exciting aspects of this 'power-tool' is that it is so simple to manage for the newspaper or journalist. Newspapers do not require expensive mainframe computers to get 'on-line', fairly unsophisticated PCs are adequate. And the reporter doing research can easily access one of the search engines on the Internet (e.g. *Lycos* or *Yahoo*). By entering a key word or phrase, the computer will search all the available databases quickly and efficiently.

Finally, journalists who cannot access information by computer will soon become redundant. The Internet is obviously challenging traditional means of news gathering and delivery.

The influence and the abilities of the computer, will surely continue to influence the practice of journalism. You as an aspirant journalist must embrace this technology and grow with it, or you will be left behind.

5 Minute Task

> *Imagine that you are starting work as a reporter in your own local area. Apply the ideas in this chapter to your own situation and note down*
> • *where you might hear news or get good ideas for stories*
> • *who would probably be good sources of information locally*
> • *who might actually leak information sometimes and why*
> • *where you might be able to do research into records, etc.*

Conclusion

In this chapter, you have learnt how to generate ideas for a story and how to build up and evaluate your own personal sources. By now you should understand that a journalist without sources is not a journalist. Lastly, you have learnt how you can conduct your own basic research.

Suggested Reading

1. Abel, Elie, *Leaking: Who does it? Who benefits? At what cost?*, New York, Priority Press Publication, 1987.

2. Berry, Thomas Elliot, *Journalism in America*, New York, Hasting House Publishers, 1976.

3. Brooks, Brian S, *et al*, The Missouri Group, *News Reporting & Writing*, New York, St Martins Press, 4th edition, 1992.

4. Nel, Francois, *Writing for the Media*, Southern Book Publishers, 1994.

5.   Teel, Leonard R, *et al, Into the Newsroom – An introduction to journalism,* Prentice-Hall, 1983.

6.   Ward, Hiley H, *Professional Newswriting,* New York, Harcourt Brace Jovanovich Publishers, 1985.

Collecting
5   the news

Introduction

So far in this book you have looked at the journalist's job in general, and at several important aspects of that job, i.e. the ethical guide-lines a journalist uses, the nature of news and the sources of news. But you have not yet looked closely at the actual work of collecting news, the day-to-day job of the reporter. That is what this chapter is about.

Outcome

At the end of this chapter you will understand how a reporter looks for news. You will know how to make routine calls, how to get ideas for a story and how to check the facts. You will also understand how to take notes and conduct interviews so that your story covers all the essential facts.

Looking for news

The basic job of a reporter is to go out and look for news. News-papers need news and have an insatiable appetite for it. As soon as one paper goes to press [gets printed] the process of gathering news starts all over again.

Although news is everywhere, the search for news must be highly organised. A reporter must search for news, check it for accuracy, and write it in a way that makes it exciting and readable. You need to develop a specific ability to do this well.

Technology has changed the way a story passes from reporter to published page. As you have seen, it has made huge new stores of information easily available to reporters. It is also true that the reporters of the future will have to be able to do jobs that they did not do in the past. Already, reporters are playing a greater role in the layout and design of the pages that they work on. With the appearance of digital cameras, more reporters will probably need photographic skills. Already, a local newspaper group has purchased a number of laptop computers that are connected to high quality digital cameras and cellular telephones. So the reporter of the future could write the story and take the necessary pictures. This reporter could then use a modem built into the laptop computer to download the photos and story into the newspaper page directly from the scene of the story. You can imagine how sportswriters could use this technology very effectively.

New technology gets the news to the reader much faster, but it has not affected the basic work of a reporter on a local story. The reporter still has to go out and look for the news. In Chapter 4 you read about ideas for building up and evaluating sources of news. Now you can read about how to work with these sources when you are looking for stories and following them up.

5 Minute Task

Picture yourself as a local reporter about to start the day's work. Your news editor has told you to find a story or stories yourself. Use what you know already and develop some ideas on the following:
* *What would you do first?*
* *With little time to spend, what other methods would you use to try to get ideas?*
* *Once you are very busy following up on some good ideas, how would you treat an unexpected tip-off about something quite different?*
Now read on.

Routine calls and contacts

Routine calls are the lifeblood of a newspaper. Every newspaper uses a system of regular calls to people who are known (or likely) to be sources of news, for example, police, MPs, hospitals, hotels and sports officials. You can make these calls personally or by telephone. Your golden rule is to make your network of routine calls as wide as possible. Smaller community newspapers rely strongly on their network of routine calls. They would struggle for information without them. Routine calls need a special technique to get the information and co-operation that you want. Firstly, give your name and newspaper. Then give your contact a little guidance to help him/her remember events that may be important. *Don't* just say, *Do you have anything for us?* Remember also that when you speak to organisations such as the police you should ensure that your contact is authorised to speak to the press.

As well as your regular routine calls, you should keep a list of contacts that you may call less often but who may give useful information when you need it. Encourage these contacts by making them feel important to your newspaper. Persuade them not to wait for you to contact them but rather to approach you as soon as they have some useful information. A good list of contacts will become your most valuable asset as a reporter. It will allow you to get straight to a story and save you many frustrating phone calls.

Tip-offs

Your daily routine calls will bring you many ideas for new stories and lead to new contacts. For example, your routine call to the owner or barman of a large shebeen may lead to a tip-off that an interesting personality will be at the shebeen tonight. Or they may have overheard someone talking about a new and interesting development. These tip-offs may lead to nothing, but never ignore the person who approaches you with information, even if you are busy. Of course, it may be that the person wishes only to cause trouble or to get free publicity (we discussed the possible motives of tipsters in Chapter 4). But on the other hand, he/she may have some important information that no other reporter or newspaper has picked up.

Don't forget that these willing informants may be providing real news, the lifeblood of your newspaper. If you get arrogant and feel that you can do without them, you may be asking for your downfall.

How to get ideas for a story

In Chapter 4 you read about a large variety of ways to generate ideas and keep them flowing. How will you chase stories from day to day on your beat? As you call your contacts, don't imagine that ideas for stories will come only from other people. Your own sharp observation will probably bring you the best stories. *Develop a habit of questioning everything.* By doing so you will find many unanswered questions.

Let us take an example: the workers at an organisation that pays very well are on strike for a 20% wage increase and management is only offering 15%, which is 5% above the inflation rate. These workers already take home a minimum of R3 000. Teachers and the police are also calling for a wage increase, but the government is only prepared to give them 8%, which is well below the inflation rate. Currently the lowest paid teachers and police officers are taking home less than R1 000 per month. You notice that the major trade unions are backing the workers of this organisation in their wage demands but are strangely silent about the demands of the teachers and the police. *Why?* The answer to this question may provide very interesting reading.

Radio and TV programmes provide plenty of ideas for stories. Something that is mentioned even briefly on these media could affect your readers and the community you live in. Another source of ideas is *your own newspaper.* Follow up on the topics that are of current interest in your area to get inspiration for a new story. For example, *Cape Town to host the 2004 Olympic Games* – What do the people in your city or area think? – What are the likely spin-offs and benefits for *your* region?

Read your opposition newspapers and newspapers from other regions. You may find a story about your area that your newspaper missed. You could try to follow up on the story but provide more depth than the original story did. National news may have news with a local echo, for example, news about trade missions abroad which involves local businessmen or news about national sports teams which involves local players, and so on.

Scan minutes of council meetings (or meetings of other local bodies) to look for obscure items, e.g. *R2 million to be written off.* Ask yourself, *Why? What does the R2 million represent?*

 **5 Minute Task**

> *Now imagine that your news editor has given you an assignment.*
> • *You don't know anything about the background to this story. What should you do?*
> • *You have to attend a meeting for the story. How can you get an efficient, accurate record of what happens there?*
> • *You must conduct an interview with one of the speakers after the meeting. Serious accusations have been made about this person. How will you handle his/her in the interview?*

Check the facts first

After you have been given an assignment by the news editor or chief reporter, it is up to you to produce the story. In order to produce a well-written, accurate and fair story, it is important that you understand exactly what is expected of you and that you find all the relevant facts. Your first task is to *check all the cutting files* that are relevant to your story. Using the cutting files should be the most basic routine task for a reporter. You don't want the sub-editor to reject your story because it has already been covered. Don't take too long with these preliminaries, as you have a story to write.

Another warning: *do not assume that a cutting from your own newspaper will always be accurate.* Often cuttings contain mistakes. If that information is used again and the new story becomes a cutting the inaccuracy gets perpetuated [continued].

Taking notes

Accurate note-taking is one of the most important and necessary skills a reporter must learn. The most important thing to learn is to *take down only what is relevant and not everything that is said.* Not only will you save yourself a lot of time but your notes will be far more accurate.

Secondly, do not rely on your memory, it may let you down when you least expect it and cause you and your newspaper professional embarrassment.

There are some other problems that commonly interfere with accuracy and relevance. For example, you may not fully understand what is being said and therefore you may record it incorrectly. Or you may not understand the full context of some of the remarks made (that is, the background and the details of the situation). Your own biases could then interfere with the message. Another problem that could arise is that you may not be sure what is relevant and what isn't until you have written down information and reviewed it.

WRITE AS FAST AS
YOU CAN!!

Some of these problems will be reduced or solved as you become more practised and build up your background knowledge. You can also use the following techniques to take good notes, keep them safe and ensure that they are easy to work with later:

1. *Write as fast as you can.* Learn shorthand or (at the very least) speed writing, and make use of symbols and abbreviations for certain words, e.g. # for number, & for and, @ for at, etc.
2. *Listen for signs that will tell you that the speaker is making a new or important point.* He/she may raise or lower his/her

voice, or pause for some time. Or he/she may use a word or phrase like: ... *an important/significant/key/vital/crucial aspect...; or, firstly... secondly... finally; or, ...in a nutshell; ...to put it quite plainly; ...my main contention is,* etc. Of course, these are English examples, but the same kind of signals could apply in other languages.

3. *Remember you cannot get everything down.* Two reports of the same speech may be very different, not because either of the reports is inaccurate but because the different reporters had different ideas about what was important in the speech.

4. *Label your notes* and make sure that you record the person's full name, the date and the time.

5. *Write your name and telephone number in your notebook* so that if you happen to lose it, the person who finds it can return it to you.

6. *If possible, use a tape recorder,* especially in question and answer type interviews. However, one problem with taped interviews is that you may get overloaded with information so that you try to use everything in your story.

7. *Always make sure that you have a spare pen and pencil handy.* The one advantage of the notebook over the tape recorder is that notebooks never have dead batteries or run out of tape.

8. *When you are taking notes at any function, try to stay until the end.* Think of the disgrace of explaining to your news editor why your story contains no mention of the dramatic incident at the end of the function (probably reported in a rival newspaper).

And here are some guidelines for you when you work with your notes later:

1. *Review your notes as soon as possible after the interview.* Your memory and ability to read your untidy handwriting may not be too good a few days later.

2. If the speaker refers to some published fact, **check the reference afterwards**. Do not accept the speaker's word.

3. If the speaker quoted someone or attacked someone not present, **give the other person the opportunity to respond** to the attack.

Dealing with people in interviews

Anonymous quotes in your story will not convince readers, so it is important to try and persuade anyone that you interview to let you use his/her name. However, take care not to become intrusive or cause embarrassment. The *Code of Conduct* Section 6 reads:

> *Subject to justification by overriding consideration of public interest, a journalist shall do nothing which entails intrusion into private grief and distress.*

A journalist should always try to be courteous. Explain what you wish to know and do not ask questions in an aggressive or demanding manner.

Similarly, it is not a journalist's job to be the bearer of bad news. That is the job of the police. When dealing with people who have just received a shock or bad news, be patient and sympathetic. If you are unwelcome, leave and return at a more opportune time.

However, you may have to be more forceful when you are dealing with people against whom allegations have been made. Make sure that you point out that it is in their best interest to make a comment rather than let a one-sided story go to press.

Always try to interview face to face. People are not comfortable being interviewed over the telephone, especially about a sensitive issue. Interviews in person also allow you to get to know your source better, which may assist you in the future. Always make an appointment where possible.

Remember to keep confidentiality but do try to persuade your source that it is better to go on the record. Always bear in mind Section 7

of the *Code of Conduct,* which reads: *A journalist shall protect
confidential sources of information.* If you are asked to keep the story
out of the press, do not agree or make any promises, but say that
you will pass on the request to the editor. Do not be fobbed off, put
your questions across just the same.

If you are dealing with a controversy, be sure to get all sides of the
story. If you encounter someone who is reluctant to speak, point out
how much damage a one-sided story could do. It is essential to get
all sides of a story because that will safeguard against the inaccuracy
of prejudiced sources. A one-sided story can lead to accusations of
bias and the possibility of legal action.

It is essential to be *thorough* in your approach to all aspects of your
work. As you write your story, try to answer all the questions that a
reader could ask. Make sure you have all the pertinent details of all
the people you interviewed, and contact them again if necessary.
If somebody claims an event is recent, find out *how* recent: did it
happen an hour ago, yesterday, a month ago? Make sure you
answer the 5Ws and 1H, i.e. Who?, Why?, Where?, When?, What?,
and How? Chapter 9 will tell you more about this aspect. You need
the facts for your story, they are essential.

 # Conclusion

The most basic job of a reporter is to go out and look for news. You
must search for news, check it for accuracy, and write it in a way that
makes it exciting and readable. Every newspaper has a system of
regular calls that are its lifeblood. The best source of stories is usually
yourself using your own powers of observation. Journalists must learn
to question everything. In order to produce a well-written, accurate
and fair story you must understand exactly what is expected of you
and you must get all the relevant facts. Accurate note-taking is an
essential skill for a reporter. Take down only what is relevant and not
everything that is said. Take care to be thorough in your approach to
all aspects of your work. Try to answer all the questions that a reader
will ask when you write your story.

Suggested Reading

1. Berry, Thomas Elliot, *Journalism in America,* New York, Hasting House Publishers, 1976.

2. Brooks, Brian S, *et al,* The Missouri Group, *News Reporting & Writing,* New York, St Martins Press, 4th edition, 1992.

3. Harris, Geoffrey, *Journalism Media Manual – Practical Newspaper Reporting,* 2nd ed, Focal Press, 1993.

4. Nel, Francois, *Writing for the Media,* Southern Book Publishers, 1994.

5. Teel, Leonard R, *et al, Into the Newsroom – An introduction to journalism,* Prentice-Hall, 1983.

6. Ward, Hiley H, *Professional Newswriting,* New York, Harcourt Brace Jovanovich, 1985.

Learning about

6   arguments

Introduction

As you read through this book, you are probably developing ideas about what news is and where to find it. You have read about why people might want to offer a reporter certain information. You may even be imagining how you can go out there and collect the news without breaking the ethical 'rules' that journalists must observe.

This chapter asks you to look more closely at what actually happens when you interview that businessperson or local government official, or cover that political meeting, or read up recent news stories to get background on the events you are covering. *Be sceptical* I have advised you, in other words, question everything, don't assume that what you are hearing is the truth, the whole truth and nothing but the truth. But how do you develop skill at separating the gold of truth from the dross [waste] of lies, half-truths or distortions?

As a reporter you will listen endlessly to others putting forward their plans, their policies, their points of view, their explanations for their actions, etc. In other words, you will hear people arguing their cases. Also, they will often be trying to out-argue someone else with a different case or point of view. For this reason, it is important that you understand how *argument* works. That is what this chapter is about.

Outcome

At the end of this chapter, you should be able to recognise arguments and make sense of them. You should also know how to construct clear and logical arguments yourself.

5 Minute Task

Find the leader page in any newspaper. Quickly read through the editorial or one of the leader articles on that page.
• Can you find the main viewpoint being offered in the article?
• Do you agree with the writer on this, or not? Why/why not?

Do journalists really need training in argument?

You would probably agree that a good journalist must be able to think and write clearly and logically. But would you go as far as Anthony Serafini suggests, in the following statement from his article *Philosophy and Journalistic Education*?:

> "...journalists should have more training in philosophy rather than other disciplines such as economics and history because philosophy is, in the essence, concerned with the cultivation of critical reasoning skills, which are also, presumably, important requisites of journalistic competence. In particular, journalists could benefit from coursework in logic, which directly teaches reasoning skills such as those involved in making sound (deductive as well as inductive) inferences and in avoiding logical fallacies." [24.] [A fallacy is an argument based on illogical or false reasoning.]

It may not be possible for all journalists to get detailed training in philosophical logic. But as a journalist, you should learn to develop and defend your own ideas and views, and respond to the ideas and views of others, in a logical and systematic manner. In other words, you must learn to think critically.

A good example of this practice is sports journalist Thomas Kwenaite, who writes for *The Independent* on Saturday. He has some very strong views about how soccer should be run in South Africa. Kwenaite studies South Africa's soccer administration, decides on its strengths and weaknesses and then gives his opinion on what he believes should be changed. For example, he might argue that the system is basically sound but the people who administer it are unsuitable. Kwenaite will look for examples within the administration to advance and strengthen his argument. In other words, he thinks critically and forms his own reasoned opinion.

One of the basics we require as journalists is thus to be able to work with arguments. But what is an argument? An argument could be: a reason advanced/offered by someone; a reasoning process; an exchange of views. Below we will try to explore the nature of arguments a little. This chapter, however, does certainly not discuss all aspects of arguments. For that, you would have to do a course in philosophy.

What is an argument?

In order to make sense or meaning of what we wish to argue we must first learn to think with arguments. We call this thinking with arguments, critical thinking. Critical thinking demands that we support or give reasons for the claims we make.

The are two different types of argument. Firstly we can talk of an argument which is really a quarrel, that is, a heated verbal clash followed by strained or broken relations between the participants. Secondly, we can refer to an argument where someone makes a claim which he/she supports with reasons, these reasons may challenge or contradict another person's claims which are equally supported by reasons. There is no need for the argument to get heated. Because both parties have supplied supporting reasons for their claims, the argument can be settled by reasoning with each other, similar to the process in a court of law.

Making sense

In order to make sense of an argument it is important to understand what the other person is saying. We have to make meaning of that communication. This is a fundamental of communication, i.e. message sent equals message received. You will have to make meaning in this way throughout your studies and beyond your studies. It is basically a life-skill that we all have to master.

You can see arguments as patterns of meaning. If we want to understand an argument we need to discover its pattern and decide what all the different parts mean and how they fit together. Basically, this is how detectives work when they visit the scene of a crime. They collect all evidence and then try to put meaning to it. Each individual piece of evidence won't solve the crime. The detectives therefore try to develop a pattern of meaning from all the evidence together, so they can understand what happened.

Understanding the parts and the whole

Understanding is something that we have to work at, it is not something we are born with. Let us look at an example. If I tell you to get up from your chair and to open the window, you will understand exactly what I want you to do. However, if I told you the same thing in Chinese you would not understand because you probably do not understand Chinese. In order to follow the instruction you needed to be able to make sense of my instruction, i.e. you needed to understand each word and the sentence as a whole.

When we put together patterns of meaning so that we can understand the whole argument it is called synthesis. To understand arguments in this way is to synthesise meaning. We can also do the opposite when we break down an argument into its different parts. We call this form of reasoning analysis. This is a little like the process when your car breaks down and you take it to a mechanic. The mechanic understands how the car works and will analyse the problem and then begin to repair it.

As a good student journalist you are already aware of how important it is for you to have a good grasp of the vocabulary and structure of English. Words are the basic building blocks of any language and we use different words to express ideas and emotions. In order to do this we structure the words into phrases and sentences. Journalists use words in special ways to achieve meaning and understanding for their readers. Words, phrases and sentences have very specific meanings so they must be used with care if you want people to understand your communication correctly. That is why all journalists must use good dictionaries and a thesaurus. These books give us the exact meaning of the words we use.

So, before we can analyse or synthesise an argument we must know the exact meaning of what the speaker/writer is saying; and the only way we can achieve this is by asking questions.

How do we recognise an argument?

An argument is a group of statements, supported by reasoning, that together make a particular claim. This claim is the main point being made. The reasons which support the claim are there to convince or persuade others that the claim is true. These reasons which support the main claim are called *premises*.

As a journalist, you will regularly have to decide whether different propositions [claims about what is true] that people make are true or not. In order to develop your critical thinking skills, you should learn to ask the following questions as a regular routine:
- *What is being said/argued/claimed/proposed?*
- *Why is it being said/argued/claimed/proposed?*
- *Do I agree/disagree?*
- *Why do I agree/disagree?*

Thus, we must question critically what is being said and then question ourselves on why we agree or disagree with it.

We may have to ask ourselves whether someone is actually trying to persuade us and/or others to accept a particular viewpoint. Certain give-away words do indicate that an argument has been made. These words are called *conclusion indicators*. Here are some examples.

- Conclusion indicators: *Accordingly...; and so...; I conclude that...; it is evident...; it follows that...; therefore...; thus....*

- *Premise indicators* signal to us that a reason is being offered in support of a claim or proposition.

- Premise indicators: *because...; for...; for the reason that...; given that...; granted that...; in the light of...; since....*

When we read or listen (and as journalists we read and listen a lot), it is important to be on the lookout for arguments. Is a claim being made? Has the claim been supported by sound reasons? Are we persuaded or convinced?

Our own arguments: making our meaning clear

You already know the basics about how to construct arguments properly if you have read the above. But confusion can still arise over the words we use. How can we make our meaning clear and avoid confusion in our statements? The best method is to use definitions. A definition is the explanation of a word or words by use of other words.

By doing this we can get clarity on the word or words used and also improve our vocabulary. Then we can steadily and increasingly avoid vagueness and ambiguity. Vagueness occurs when the meaning is not made clear enough. If an argument is vague it cannot be considered a good argument. Ambiguity on the other hand happens when there are two or more different possible meanings for the same word or words, and they are used in such a way that it is not clear which one is meant.

5 Minute Task

> Reread the article you analysed for the first task in this chapter.
> - Do you still have the same view of the claim the writer is making in the article?
> - Do you still have the same response to the claim, i.e. agreement/disagreement?
> - If your view has changed, why has it changed? Is the change a result of what you have learnt about arguments?

Conclusion

You should now have a basic idea of how to recognise arguments you read or hear, and how to apply a critical understanding to these arguments. You should also have a basic knowledge of how to construct clear and logical arguments yourself. As you gain practical experience, you should be able to apply this critical thinking ability while you are interviewing someone or taking notes at meetings and other events.

Suggested Reading

1. Serafini, Anthony, *Philosophy and Journalistic Education; Philosophical Issues in Journalism,* Oxford University Press, New York, 1992.

The skill of
7   interviewing

Introduction

M any journalists would argue that you can't separate news-gathering from interviewing. They are quite correct. Interviewing is an important part of news gathering. We have chosen to deal with interviewing as a separate chapter simply because it is also a specific skill that all reporters need to master if they wish to be successful journalists. However, when you are revising you should read Chapters 5 and 6 together.

Outcome

At the end of this chapter, you will know how to prepare for an interview and how to plan, conduct and record a successful interview.

The importance of interviews

Almost all news stories are the result of personal interviews. Even the reporter who is an eyewitness to an event must talk to other eyewitnesses to clarify facts and to get different viewpoints. *"Information is the merchandise of a journalist."* [25.] We collect facts, weave the facts into information and then sell it to our readers. The quality and richness of the information we sell depends much on how we have worked with the people who can release that information to us.

As journalists, we must be careful not to become wooed [charmed, persuaded] by the people we interview. Most public figures are charming when you get them into the interview situation, but that doesn't mean that they will give you the information you need. As Nel says, *"Successful politicians did not get to be successful politicians by being dumb enough to tell reporters the truth, or tell reporters much of anything."* [26.]

Interviews take many different forms. They may be impromptu [unprepared] or planned; co-operative or antagonistic; exclusive to one reporter or open to all, as in a press conference. The reporter may need to use different approaches and techniques to suit the different types of interview, the different situations in which they can take place and the different possible aims for the interview in his/her own mind.

Interviewing is a difficult business, so you should do all you can to ensure that you control those aspects that you *can* control. For example, you should have a goal, *What do you want from the interview?* There is a great scene in Lewis Carroll's book *Alice in Wonderland* where Alice is lost and asks a Cheshire cat for directions:

> *"Would you tell me, please, which way I ought to go from here?"* asks Alice.
> *"That depends a good deal on where you want to go,"* replies the cat.
> *"I don't much care where,"* says Alice.
> *"Then it doesn't much matter which way you go,"* is the reply.
> *"So long as I get somewhere,"* Alice adds as an explanation.
> *"Oh, you are sure to do that,"* grins the cat.

You need to have more direction than Alice did! Therefore, you will probably accept that you need to learn much and practise more to become a skilled interviewer.

10 Minute Task

> *Think about interviewing two different kinds of people:*
> * *A local politician involved in a controversy.*
> * *A visiting international pop star/actor/fashion designer.*
> * *In each case, how would you prepare for the interview?*
> * *What sort of questions would you ask these different types of interviewee?*
> * *How would you get the confidence of each of these people?*

Preparation, preparation

The foundation of a successful interview is thorough planning *before* you ask the first question. Do your homework by finding out as much about your subject as possible. You could insult the person by conducting your interview cold [unprepared], whereas if you have a thorough knowledge of his/her past and achievements you will certainly win his/her respect. If you can't avoid going in unprepared, admit this openly, and put yourself at the interviewee's mercy. Don't try to bluff your way out, you probably won't succeed. Even when you have planned and researched well, interviews seldom go as they are supposed to.

Research

You may have the frustrating experience of being told to do research, yet nobody tells you how to go about it. What are we trying to do when we *research* something? Usually we are trying to do one of the following: explain behaviour, predict behaviour or determine the reasons for behaviour. How you actually do your research depends of course on what kind of assignment you have been given.

However, reporters generally use two types of research: *asking informal sources* and *desk research*. It is a good idea to get advice from other journalists who may have done a similar story. These are your *informal sources*. Then it is time for your desk research.

Before you begin, write down what your *hypothesis* is and what you expect to find out. Your *hypothesis* means your idea of what has taken place. It is an idea that you have formed by reasoning carefully, but you are not totally certain that it is true.

Your hypothesis will help to focus you in your interview, but you should still try to research with an open mind. If you hold your hypothesis too inflexibly, you may miss something that isn't part of your hypothesis but *is* nevertheless relevant to your story.

A good example of this problem is the young *BBC* journalist who was sent to interview the late Bob Marley's press agent about his next concert. Her entire interview was taped, much to her embarrassment and her editor's anger. It went something like this:

Reporter: *Could you tell me when Bob Marley will*
               be arriving in London?
Press Agent: *Bob died fifteen minutes ago.*
Reporter: *So the concert's off, then?*
Press Agent: *Bob died fifteen minutes ago.*
Reporter: *Could you tell me about Bob's next record?*
Press Agent: *BOB DIED fifteen minutes ago – and this*
               interview is now over!

This young reporter was sitting on the scoop of a lifetime but she was so focused on asking her prepared questions that she did not listen and take in what she was being told.

When you have developed your hypothesis, you should visit your newspaper's cutting library and then the various data banks and other media available to you. You will almost certainly need to search the Internet, too.

If you are to do a *news* story, go first to the cuttings library and review all the cuttings on the subject of the story rather than only those about the personality you must interview. Naturally, if you must do a *profile* you should concentrate on that personality's interests, friends, career, schooling, etc. For an *investigative* story, you will have to concentrate on all aspects. Remember, keep asking the basic question of all journalists – *Why?*

Time management

It is important to plan your time. How much time do you have to do your research, plan and conduct your interview, do any follow-up research and then write your story?

Arriving late for an interview is a cardinal sin. Time is precious, some celebrities will allocate you a particular time, say between 11h00 and 11h15. If you arrive ten minutes late you will have to conduct your interview in the remaining five minutes. Being late for an interview harms your professionalism and your newspaper's reputation. Your subject probably won't grant you another interview and you will have an embarrassing time explaining to your editor why you did not do the interview.

When asking for an interview, it is a good idea to state exactly how much time you require. *Do not waste time*, important people seldom have time to waste and they appreciate those who value time. If the interviewee invites you to stay longer, accept the offer only if there is still important information that you need. Otherwise you can politely decline and leave.

Formulating and phrasing questions

There are two golden rules of interviewing:

1.   Ask the question!
2.   Do not ask what you already know.

There is nothing more frustrating to an editor than to hear a reporter say: *I was going to ask* or, *I wanted to ask.* If you have done your research properly it should have led you to some questions that your readers want to know the answers to. Asking questions to which you already know the answer is a waste of valuable time.

It is a good idea to write down at least ten questions to which you require answers. But as the inexperienced BBC reporter in the 'Bob Marley' interview learned, interviews seldom go according to plan. Use your list of questions to guide you through the interview and remind you of the important points. Because you have prepared your questions, you will be more relaxed and the conversation can be natural and spontaneous.

The answer to your first question may lead to an interesting new focus, so that the rest of your questions become irrelevant. Therefore it is important to listen actively to what you are being told. Do not be afraid to ask for clarification if you do not understand something. According to Francois Nel:

> "Do not be afraid to let someone know that you are searching blindly. Many interesting details have come from simply asking, 'Is there something else you think may help me?" [27.]

The way you word your questions is most important. The structure of your questions will often determine whether your interview is a success or not. Badly phrased questions have made reporters lose many good stories. *Open-ended questions* are less direct and not so threatening for the interviewee.

What is an *open-ended* question? It is a question that requires more than a direct *yes* or *no* answer. For example, if you ask a visiting celebrity: *Did you enjoy your stay in South Africa?*, they might reply either *Yes* or *No*. Therefore you have asked a *closed* question. However if you ask: *What has impressed you most about South Africa?*, you are then inviting the celebrity to answer in a bit more detail. Such an open-ended question is far more flexible. It is a good idea to use open-ended questions at the beginning of your interview in order to get the interviewee relaxed and talking. Open-ended questions are less threatening and less direct but nevertheless probing.

Of course, there are times that you require a straight *yes* or *no* answer. Then a closed question is appropriate. However, it is important to know when to ask each type of question. You will learn this from practice and experience.

Vague questions get vague answers but specific questions are more likely to get explicit answers. Specific, probing questions also tell the interviewee that you have done your research thoroughly.

Planning and conducting the interview

An important part of good interviewing is the planning you do just before you start the actual interview. Here are some key points on this:

Talk to the correct person: Firstly, ensure that the person you are going to interview is the correct person and is able to and *authorised* to give you the information you want. You can cause a lot of trouble by approaching the wrong person. You may get a great story from a paramedic who does not fully appreciate the medical problems experienced by a patient. The paramedic is not authorised or qualified to discuss the problem and should have referred you to the doctor concerned. The paramedic gets disciplined for talking out of turn and in the end no one is satisfied. The problem with interviewing the wrong person is that you usually cause resentment. It is therefore important to go through the right channels to obtain an interview.

Choose a good time: The result of your interview has commercial value (i.e. it will help to sell your newspaper) therefore it is important to time your approach. If you phone after 10 am you will usually be well received but if you phone at 3 am for something that could have waited till later you will be greeted with anger. Always try to be courteous and make an appointment whenever possible.

Consider the place: The environment for your interview is important. Most interviews are conducted in the interviewee's office, but if you conduct the interview on neutral ground, it could give you an advantage.

Check your equipment: Before you leave for the interview make sure you have not forgotten your prepared questions, that you are adequately attired and that you have all the equipment that you will need. What equipment will you need? Spare pens and pencils, notebook, tape recorder and spare batteries. It is a good idea to make a checklist and tick them off before you go. Lastly, make sure that you are on time.

5 Minute Task

Interviewing problems
- *Brainstorm and list the problems you would expect to experience in interviews.*
- *Select two problems which seem more important than the rest.*
- *Suggest how you might prevent these problems, or how you might deal with them in the interview.*

Different approaches

Arranging an interview is usually easier said than done. Important and powerful people are usually surrounded by protective secretaries and public relations people whom you will have to get past. Sometimes you will have to deal with people who are so used to rudeness and abuse that they are always suspicious of anyone asking questions.

Let's discuss a number of approaches you may need to adopt:

Direct approach: Call the person on the telephone, introduce yourself and your newspaper and tell him/her what you want.

Begging: Sometimes you simply have to appeal to a person's sense of sympathy. This approach works best when dealing with the survivors of tragedy, *Could you please tell me where I could contact Mr Bigcheese, it's very urgent?*

The assault: This is used on reluctant interviewees. You simply ask your question as quickly and forcibly as possible, *Mr Early, you have been accused of embezzling money from the SA Rugby Union. Do you care to comment?*

Being courteous and understanding: It does no harm to be courteous, and it usually pays. It is also a great way to go about your business. People who get much abuse may feel overwhelmed by kindness and will be only too happy to talk to you, *I know there are two sides to a story and I would love to hear yours.*

The sit-in: When you get put off by one of Mr Bigcheese's protectors, simply say that you know that he is busy and you will wait until he is free. Take your lunch and a book to show that you are serious. Persistence often works but don't use this method too much.

Establishing confidence

From the moment you first meet your interviewee it is important to establish confidence with them. The interviewee must feel that they can trust you to tell their story fairly, accurately and without bias. Probably the best piece of advice you can get when it comes to dealing with people is, *be nice to people*. Try not to seem patronising but always be courteous.

Establishing rapport: A sympathetic, easy exchange between you, the journalist, and your interviewee will make or break the interview. Often the relationship is somewhere between relaxed and strained. The quality of the relationship will decide what type of co-operation you get. This can go beyond one story and affect future stories.

One of my students, who was getting her in-service training at a local newspaper, did a story on child abuse. The following week she got a telephone call from some parents whose children had been sexually abused. They liked the sensitive way she had handled the story and wanted her to tell the story of their own children's nightmare.

Listen carefully to your interviewee's response to your questions as this is an important key to how you should continue. Do not be caught off guard. If you respond too quickly to a question like, *Who told you that?*, you could reveal your confidential source without realising what you are doing.

A point on appropriate dress: Remember you can dress as you please but your source does not have to talk to you. Try to fit in with the environment. If you have to go to a State banquet then it is probably wise to dress formally. It is a good idea to check on your appearance before you leave for your interview.

Dealing with reluctant people

Some interviewees will be cordial [friendly] towards you, others will be reluctant or hostile in their response. But nearly all of them will also be *guarded* [cautious, watchful]. Usually they will request not to be quoted and they will only wish to speak off the record. Often they will only *give* the interview off the record. Always agree to the condition at the beginning of the interview, then as the interview progresses and the interviewee relaxes, try to get them to give up their *off the record* ruling. Point out that the report will be more credible [believable] if they go on the record.

Often the interviewee adds this condition at the *end* of the interview. It is a good idea to ask during the interview, maybe more than once, *I take it that I can use this?* However, if you agree to treat the interviewee's responses as off the record, *do not go back on your word.*

Often you can get a reluctant person to respond if you tell him/her that you have some viewpoints and that you would like to hear his/her thoughts. Quite often he/she will respond with, *No, it's not like that at all,* and will then tell you his/her version of events. Others are reluctant due to false modesty and wish to be coaxed into talking.

Controlling the interview

Usually the best way to start the interview is simply to ask an open-ended question like, *Can you tell me what happened?* Once your interviewee begins to talk, do not interrupt – let him/her tell the story as far as possible without your help. Only interrupt the interviewee if you need to get the *main* drift of the story clear in your mind. Ask for minor points of clarification only at the end. Don't express your personal reactions much unless the interviewee clearly expects a reaction. If he/she tells an amusing story it is a good idea to laugh.

Once the interviewee has completed his/her story, begin asking your questions. Start to probe around the main theme of the story, asking questions that will produce an interesting response. Try to get exact answers, *What do you mean by fast?* or *What were the problems you mentioned?* Ask for explanations if the answers do not make sense to you.

Interviewing is not an exact science. You ask a question but you can never be certain of the response you will receive. The more questions you ask the more likely you are to hear something interesting, but be careful not to be led astray. Remember the most important answers may come at any time during the interview.

Try to be interested in the answers you get even if they do not appear to be newsworthy. The very excited or self-important interviewee can be a problem when he/she goes off the point or continually repeats information that may not be very useful to you. However, usually he/she only needs to be prodded back on to the main theme.

Dealing with attempts to censor/vet your story

Whatever type of interview you conduct, *resist any attempt to vet or censor your copy* ['check it', 'crit' it and 'approve' it] by your interviewee. Occasionally you can make an exception where the story deals with complex technical subjects and you might have misunderstood some details. If the interviewee demands to vet the story in return for giving the interview, say that you will put the request to the editor. If you do ask for clarification, make it clear, as tactfully as possible, that you want help with the facts only. That is, you are *not* asking for changes to your style or wording.

Recording your interview and taking notes

This was discussed in some detail in Chapter 5. In that chapter we emphasised accurate note-taking. Here are a few more tips on managing the recording of your interviews:

Your note-pad: The most convenient note-pad is a hard back spiral note-pad that can be held in one hand. It is easier to hold if you have to stand and take notes. People are also less daunted [intimidated] by the sight of a small, unobtrusive note-pad. Number, date and keep your old note-pads for later reference – you never know when you may have to refer to an old interview.

Taping your interviews: Nowadays, most reporters also tape their interviews if the interviewee does not mind. The taped interview has a number of advantages:

1.   Total and accurate recall.
2.   You can observe the interviewee's reactions.
3.   The interviewee will be quoted correctly.

A problem with the taped interview is that you can get too much information and it takes time to wade through it all. I personally prefer to use a tape recorder to interview because I feel it leads to accuracy. But I like to take notes as well in order to remember those things that stand out as important.

 # Conclusion

Interviewing is not an exact science. In order to get a good interview it is important to do research, plan the questions and ensure that you control the interview process from beginning to end.
You cannot allow the progress of an interview to be left to chance.

Suggested Reading

1.   Berry, Thomas Elliot, *Journalism in America*, New York, Hasting House Publishers, 1976.

2.   Brooks, Brian S, *et al*, The Missouri Group, *News Reporting & Writing*, New York, St Martins Press, 4th edition, 1992.

3.   Harris, Geoffrey, *Journalism Media Manual – Practical Newspaper Reporting*, 2nd ed, pp 6-19 Focal Press, 1993.

4.   Nel, Francois, *Writing for the Media*, Southern Book Publishers, 1994.

5.   Teel, Leonard R, *et al, Into the Newsroom – An introduction to journalism,* Prentice-Hall, 1983.

6.   Ward, Hiley H, *Professional Newswriting,* New York, Harcourt Brace Jovanovich Publishers, 1985.

Newspaper
8 language

Introduction

Our school system seems to produce many common errors and the quality of English teaching is poor. As a result you may find that you need to work on producing clear, grammatical newspaper language. This chapter cannot handle this subject fully, but it will give you a clear understanding of what *newspaper language* is and what you should know in order to construct a well written article.

Outcome

At the end of this chapter, you will know the importance of clear concise English. You will know why journalists avoid writing long sentences and you will understand the basic grammar, punctuation and style rules that newspaper language follows.

5 Minute Task

Discuss with a fellow-student or colleague:
What kind of language should be used in newspapers, and why?
If you use English as a journalist, which English should you use?

Why clear and concise English is important

For the journalist, clear and concise English is important because accurate communication is important. In other words, the message we want to send to our readers must be the message they receive. Our writing should be incisive [sharp and clear] so that there is no doubt about what we are trying to say. People from many different educational and cultural backgrounds read newspapers. The content must therefore be easy to understand for everybody.

However, we need to understand what language is and what English means to us and our readers before we can easily decide what kind of language we should use. Hartley 1982 describes the importance of language in our lives:

> *"...through language we learn how we should act; within the framework that it establishes we find, explore and understand our own individuality, and through it we gain access to social relationships."* [28.]

He also points out the ways in which language can play a part in structuring and controlling our world:

> *"... language is also a form of social control, because people generally voluntarily submit to its rules and conventions. It is also through language that we learn to accept the social forces and institutions around us as natural."* [29.]

In short, we live through language. Language and the way it is used is therefore enormously important to those people who read or write newspapers. Because English is the language of choice for mass communication in most of Africa, it is essential that journalists learn to communicate effectively in English. English is a dynamic, changing, growing language, a language that is constantly being used for hundreds of different purposes by millions of people. Different people are adapting English in different ways as they use it daily. So how do we find an English that is acceptable to different readers?

One answer is that we should accept and even celebrate the changes that happen to English as our people use it. However, isn't there a problem that what is English to some people may be unacceptable to (or not even understood by) others? We therefore need to use an English that everyone will understand and accept.

Some reporters use the following test: ask yourself whether anyone would speak the way you have written. If the answer is *No*, delete the passage and start again. As Harris says:

> *"Ordinary speech is a good guide for the correctness of newspaper English, though obviously you can rarely tell a newspaper story exactly as you would tell it to a friend: you have to manage with fewer words."* [30.]

And of course, you need to cut out any forms of English that are understood by you and your friend but not by many other people.

You could also use the English of radio and television news bulletins as a guide. Newspapers need a text that is similar to the broadcast news reader's text – short sentences that read easily and are quickly understood.

Sentence length

Some people have the strange belief that the longer a sentence is, the better the writing must be. This is a very mistaken idea. The long sentence is usually difficult to follow, unlikely to flow smoothly and very likely to bore the reader to sleep. So, what can we do? The first golden rule is: *Look very suspiciously at every sentence longer than 24 words and double check any sentence longer than 30 words.* Simply don't write sentences longer than 24 words unless absolutely necessary. Your sentences must be simple and clear which means short.

Journalists normally have to write under pressure and although it is possible to write clear long sentences, it is not easy to write clear long sentences in a hurry. It is usually possible to break a long rambling sentence into two short, easier-to-read sentences. Try not to make your sentences so short that they sound like a machine gun.

Try to be *democratic* with your thoughts and sentences. That is, *one thought, one sentence.* Write in a direct manner. Use verbs rather than verbal nouns. It is better to say *'as he scored'* than *'when scoring'.*

Using the right words

Every journalism student should have a good dictionary, a thesaurus and a dictionary of synonyms and antonyms. These three books should be the most used books they own. No journalist should write without these three books at hand, and they should be referred to constantly. Sometimes the change in meaning between two words with similar meanings is slight but important and we can embarrass ourselves if we don't use the right word at the right time.

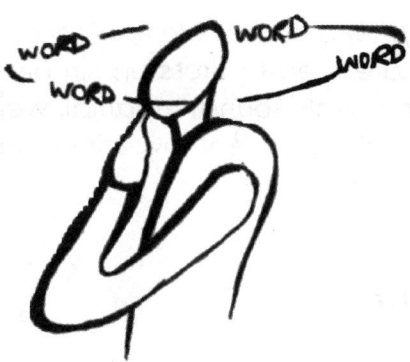

Let's take an example: You have received some information and you are not certain how to describe it. The first word you think of is *report* – you received a report. A *report* implies ... *some ground for belief unless specifically qualified as being false or untrue.* No, you feel that the information you received is not so certain. What about *rumour? Rumour* suggests a report that flies about and gathers detail as it spreads, but has no clear source and no clear-cut evidence that it is true. Again, you decide that this does not fit your information. *Gossip*, perhaps? That sounds better. *Gossip* applies to *idle, often personal, chatter that is chief source and also means a propagation of rumours or reports.* No, that is not it, it wasn't just idle, personal chatter. What about *hearsay? Hearsay* stresses the *source* of a rumour or report, as *something heard rather than something seen or known directly.* When the word 'hearsay' is used to describe evidence, it suggests that there is only indirect and imperfect knowledge of the facts. You decide this word fits – what you received was not a report, rumour or gossip, but hearsay.

Journalists owe it to their readers to choose their words with care and caution. It is simply not acceptable to choose a word we think is 'close enough'. We must rather select the word that conveys the meaning *exactly.*

We often look for words to spice up our writing, e.g. to make it more varied and interesting to read. One word that we like to change is the word 'said'. Don't be too afraid of using *said* quite a lot, as the words we use in its place are often much less suitable. Be careful of using *stated, declared, claimed, uttered,* or *continued* because their meaning might change the tone of your sentence.

Similarly, words like *phenomenon, element, effective, virtual, facilitate, utilise* and *liquidate* are used to dress up simple statements and to make biased judgements sound impartial, well-informed and reasonable. For example, a current favourite in the media is *radical elements*. Avoid words like these.

Words and idioms

Words are the main tools of the journalist. You must therefore take an active interest in words and their uses. As we have already emphasised, you should keep a good dictionary, a thesaurus and a dictionary of synonyms and antonyms available. Lively, *idiomatic* English that is appropriate to the subject and the occasion, will add to your writing and make it memorable or at least not forgettable.

Words, phrases and even slang expressions that are commonly used can be used in newspapers, although you should use slang only when quoting someone else's words. (Dress words in inverted commas only if you wish to emphasise that this is the actual word somebody used.) Avoid exaggeration. Use word and *idiom* to fit the circumstances you are writing about. What is an *idiom*? It is a phrase or word cluster that is specific to a language (e.g. English). Its meaning is not just a combination of the meanings of each of the words which make it up. Its meaning fits the whole phrase only. Expressions like *pass out, in order to*, or *give way* are all idioms.

Ask yourself whether the words and idioms you have used really do capture the spirit and style of the event that you are describing. Use words and idioms with taste and tact, even when they are the right ones. Remember to use idioms with special care. Idioms do bring liveliness to your writing, and many idioms are familiar even to readers whose mother-tongue is not English. However, certain idioms may make text hard to understand for some readers, although this may not be obvious to you until you think about it.

Getting the tone right

An important aspect of style is *tone*. Tone shows how the writer sees his/her relationship with the reader, e.g. a writer may write:

Answer immediately.
   OR
Could I ask you for an answer?
   OR
I would be grateful if you would answer as soon as possible.

You can offend a person if the tone of your writing does not accurately reflect your relationship with that person. The first two examples would be used only if you were superior in status to the reader.

Each newspaper has its own tone. Some newspapers use a quite informal tone and take many opportunities to address the reader directly, (e.g. *We're asking you, the reader, to tell us what you think about...*). Others maintain a fairly formal tone, more distanced from the reader. You will need to understand and conform to the tone of your newspaper. Some journalists may be responsible for a section or column, (e.g. in the entertainment pages) which deliberately strike a different tone from the tone in the main news and feature pages.

Contractions, slang, jargon and foreign words

Slang, like *jargon* and *technical language*, is the special or private language of a particular group. Jargon is used mainly to impress others and slang is used mainly to mark a group and its members as special or exclusive. Students use slang to exclude parents, lecturers and other non-students from their communication. Because slang causes strong emotional reactions, it can bring members of the group closer together. It evokes [raises, calls up] feelings of warmth and loyalty to the group from members, but it evokes hostile feelings from non-members. You should therefore avoid using slang when your readers do not share group membership. It is best to use ordinary, common speech to solve stylistic problems. Therefore, do not be afraid to use contractions [shortened forms] such as *I'm, didn't, haven't, can't* and so on. These are all commonplace in normal speech.

Jargon is the use of pretentious [show-off] words usually linked with a particular occupation or status. Surfers use jargon to describe surfing conditions and manoeuvres that non-surfers can't understand. Students may do the same in their spoken language. Jargon can annoy or puzzle readers in a way similar to the way slang alienates them. However, do not confuse jargon with *technical language*. Technical language can be legitimate and necessary for expressing specific meanings of concepts in computer technology, law, medicine, etc. But the use of technical language is only appropriate when writing for specialist readers. Specialised technical terms are inappropriate for a *lay* audience [non-specialist readers]. You should try to find terms that readers will understand better. Remember, our function as journalists is to communicate to people of varying education.

Foreign words bring the same difficulties as technical words do. Although the use of foreign words impresses some audiences, there is no place for them in an English newspaper. Use only those foreign words which have been accepted totally in the language. Words such as *compére* and *entrée* are now part of normal English.

Correct word order

The correct word order in a sentence is the basis of English sentence grammar. It is important to keep words together that belong together. Some languages have relatively free word order but this is generally not so with English. For example, *The boy loves the girl* and *The girl loves the boy* have quite different meanings. In this case, changing the word order changes the meaning of the sentence entirely.

Students frequently have difficulty with the placing of the following adverbs: *also, even, just, merely, only, simply.* Ambiguity [two different possible meanings] can result if these words are not placed near the word(s) they modify, e.g. *I only lent him my notes.*

It is not clear whether the notes were lent to one person only or whether the notes were the only thing that was lent. The following versions are unambiguous and therefore better. *I lent only him my notes. I lent him only my notes.*

Commas are useful and show which words should be read together. However, a sentence with too many commas is difficult to read. The best way to deal with a sentence that needs too many commas is to break the sentence into two or more sentences.

Variety and readability

It is important to write clearly and accurately, as you know. However, if your article is quite long, it also needs to be readable – that is, *good* to read. Variety is what makes English good to read so you should avoid using the same words or using a similar sound continuously. Try to inject rhythm into your sentences. Your final sentence must reach a climax, it should not trail away into nothing.

Basic style rules

Most newspapers have a set of instructions for writing and editing copy which all journalists writing for the newspaper must conform to. As a new journalist at the newspaper or magazine, you will have to learn this stylebook off-by-heart. If every journalist on the paper knows and follows the same rules, every journalist knows exactly what is required for all aspects of the work. This includes everything from preparing copy through to writing style, grammar and also layout and design. Conformity [everyone following the same rules] is important. Firstly, conformity makes it easier for editors and subeditors to edit your work and secondly, the readers know what to expect when they open their newspapers.

Using the stylebook to avoid common style problems

Preparing your copy: First, the stylebook will give general instructions on how to prepare and store copy and how you should transfer this copy between yourself and the news editor and sub-editor. The stylebook will also give specific instructions on how you should type the article and what font and size of font you should use. Very few newspapers today use hard copy, so you will do all changes and editing on screen. All writing must conform with acceptable journalistic style.

As you prepare your copy, you should aim to give your news editor and sub-editor as little work to do as possible (and if possible no work at all) in editing your copy. Make sure that you have checked all the relevant details and have the correct spelling of all names. An important example of what to check: never forget that to most people the sweetest sounding words are their names, so don't get people's names and titles wrong.

It is not easy to keep in line with the stylebook, but it is essential, because the newspaper must conform to a style acceptable to its readers. Readers demand a high level of conformity and are very unforgiving about grammar, punctuation and spelling errors. The stylebook expresses the newspaper's attitude towards writing. In this way it counsels all journalists who write for the paper on what is expected from their copy.

Punctuation: Second, the stylebook will lay down specific instructions for punctuation. Here are some typical and useful examples:

The **period (full-stop)** must be used at the end of every sentence and with abbreviations, e.g. *Rev. Dr. P. Smith, Col. K. Ngubane, Ford Motor Co.* The period should be omitted after headlines, captions, figures and the letters standing for well-known agencies, e.g. *CNN, SABC.*

The **comma** is used in a series e.g. *He selected sweets, fruit, juice and biscuits.* The comma is used to separate unrelated adjectives, e.g. *It was a long, hard match.* The comma is used to set off an introductory element such as *However,* or *Therefore,.* The comma is used to indicate the start of a direct quotation, e.g. *He said, "I am going home to ...".*

A common error is to use the comma to join grammatically independent sentences, e.g. *These days international rugby is not sport, it is war.* This can be corrected in a number of ways:
1.   substituting the comma with a full-stop
2.   substituting the comma with a semi-colon
3.   or by linking the two sections, e.g. *These days international rugby is a war rather than a sport.*

The **apostrophe** is used to denote the possessive case of nouns, e.g. *John's* car; *Siswe's* book. An apostrophe is also used to denote a contraction or an omission, e.g. *do not* can be contracted to *don't.*

Figures: Numbers from one to ten are spelled out; numbers from 11 on may be written in their Arabic form. There are a few exceptions. Time should be written as *2:25 a.m.,* or *3:15 p.m. yesterday.* Sums of money should be written as *R12* and not *R12.00.*

Never start a sentence with an Arabic numeral and if the first word in a sentence is a number then it should be written out. If a sentence contains more than one number, one below ten and the other above, then use Arabic numerals for both, e.g. *They collected between 7 and 12 eggs.* If you are using a phrase then spell the number out, e.g. *He was a man in a million.*

The stylebook would also deal with the use of the colon, semicolon, dash, hyphen, parentheses, quotation marks, abbreviations and capitalisation.

 ## Conclusion

Although this chapter does not cover everything on this subject, it should have given you a basic understanding of what newspaper language is and what you should know in order to construct a well written article. You now know the importance of clear concise English, why journalists avoid writing long sentences and why good grammar, punctuation and style are important.

Suggested Reading

1.　Berry, Thomas Elliot, *Journalism in America,* New York, Hasting House Publishers, 1976.

2.　Brooks, Brian S, *et al,* The Missouri Group, *News Reporting & Writing,* New York, St Martins Press, 4th edition, 1992.

3.　Harris, Geoffrey, *Journalism Media Manual – Practical Newspaper Reporting,* 2nd ed, Focal Press, 1993, pp 6-19.

News
9 writing

Introduction

Journalistic writing is not as difficult as some editors or teachers of journalism may tell you. Nor is it as simple as it appears when you see it on the page. However journalistic writing is *different* from all other forms of writing that you may use, and it is your most important ability as a journalist. Journalistic writing is concise, succinct writing [writing which makes points briefly and clearly]. This style is necessary because editorial space is always limited in the modern newspaper. The space available on any day depends on the amount of advertising space sold and the newspaper needs to sell as much advertising as possible. You therefore need to learn how to say a lot in a little space, and how to give your most important information at the beginning of each story.

Outcome

By the end of this chapter, you will be able to construct a lead paragraph, using the *inverted pyramid* style, as an introduction for a news story. You will know what makes a good lead and will also be able to identify various types of leads.

Using the basic rules for news writing

The following rules will help you to make decisions about your writing not only at the beginning but throughout any news story you may write.

1. Keep your paragraphs short. Write no more than five typewritten lines per paragraph.

2. Get to the point quickly. You should normally do so in the first two or three sentences, that is, the lead.

3. Use the active voice rather than the passive. The active voice adds energy and excitement to a story.

4. Select only the most significant and relevant details.

5 Minute Task

Select an important incident that has just occurred in your town,
on your campus, etc. It should be an incident which you have
quite a lot of information about.

Imagine that you have to write about it for the local or student
newspaper. (Don't read any actual reports about it.)

Decide how you think this incident should be covered in your
chosen publication.

Write the lead paragraph(s) for the story only.

Now read on and see whether you have met the requirements
for good lead-writing.

Gathering your information

Before you start writing your story, you will of course need to gather
much information by asking routine questions. Let's consider a story
like the following: *A drunken truck driver collides with a car on the
highway and both drivers are injured.* Here are some of the questions you would need to ask when covering an event like this:

* When did the accident occur?
* When was it reported?
* Who reported it?
* How was it reported?
* How long did it take the essential services (police, paramedics,
  fire department) to respond?
* How long did it take to remove the wreckage?
* How many accidents have been attributed to the abuse of
  alchohol this year?
* How does that compare to figures in previous years?
* Were there any injuries or deaths?
* What was the damage?
* Who owned the vehicles?
* Did the drivers have comprehensive insurance?
* Was the truck driver arrested by the police?
* Will charges be filed against the truck driver?

- When will the truck driver appear in court?
- Was there anything unusual about this accident?

With all the information that such questions will uncover, you can begin to write the story.

How to begin – your first paragraph

How full of facts can we pack the first paragraph? There is much debate about this, and you will have to consider several aspects. Firstly, you as writer must be clear about what is really important and what is interesting but not so important. Secondly, the reader should see what you are writing about immediately; there must be no confusion. Finally, all the basic facts should be at the beginning of the story. Some writers try to achieve this in the first paragraph. Others use the first four or five paragraphs. Obviously, you will be able to write with better style if you do not have to pack all the most important facts into the first paragraph. We will discuss this more fully later.

Emphasising what is new and important

A news story should begin with news – something new. If there is no news why should the reader bother to read on? Think about how you would tell a friend about an accident you saw. You would get straight to the point and say something like this:

> *"I saw this terrible accident on the way to work this morning – between a truck and a car on the highway. Both the drivers were injured and they were being attended to by paramedics. It seems the truck driver had been drinking – he lost control and drove into the back of the car."*

You should use the same direct and succinct approach when you write a lead to a story.

Some articles you write will be follow-ups of earlier events. In this case you must always begin your story with a brief explanation of the previous event. But do not kill your report by reciting *all* the previous history.

Avoid beginning any story with a negative or with expressions that require words like *no, not,* or *unlikely.* If there is no news, why should the reader read on?

Writing a lead using the 5W + 1H pattern

In order to write a good lead – that is, the first one or two paragraphs of a story – you have to know what questions the story must answer. All stories must answer *the 5Ws: who, what, where, when* and *why.* Furthermore, most stories will answer the question, *How?* In the traditional news story these basic questions should be answered in the first few sentences. Although it is no longer essential that you answer all the *5Ws and 1H* in the first two sentences, it is still better to answer them as soon as possible. Let us apply this guideline to the motor accident scenario mentioned earlier:

> *"I saw this terrible accident on the way to work this morning between a truck and a car on the highway. Both the drivers were injured and they were being attended to by paramedics. The truck driver had been drinking – he lost control and drove into the back of the car."*

WHO?   That is: *Who is the action about?* In this example, the answer is *two drivers.* We may wish to name the people involved in the story. Sometimes we can use a name and title: *Education Minister Sibusiso Bengu.* We may also want to use a brief description: *A 25-year-old KwaZulu-Natal truck driver, Mr Joe Mkhize ....*

WHAT?   That is: *What happened?* In this case, *a truck and a car were involved in an accident.* Once again, this may require a small description: *A 25-year-old KwaZulu-Natal truck driver, Mr Joe Mkhize, while under the influence of alcohol, was involved in an accident when his vehicle collided with a truck.*

WHERE?   *Where did it happen?* If you fail to mention where an event occurred you could confuse and annoy readers. In this case it happened *on the highway.* However, you should be be more specific than this in a news story.

For example, you can include street addresses and landmarks. However, an address may not mean very much to many readers. You could rather point out that the incident occurred *on the southern bound highway opposite the old power station.*

If your newspaper is in Durban and the event took place in Cape Town you might use a *dateline* preceding the first paragraph, as follows:

CAPE TOWN: A 25-year-old KwaZulu-Natal truck driver, Mr Joe Mkhize, was involved in a collision with a car, while under the influence of alcohol.

WHEN?   *When did it happen? This morning.* Again, we should be a little more accurate. Usually we simply use the day of the week but sometimes we may wish to be more specific: *A 25-year-old KwaZulu-Natal truck driver, Mr Joe Mkhize, while under the influence of alcohol, was involved in an accident this morning during rush hour traffic.*

WHY?   *Why did it happen?* This is sometimes a very hard or even impossible question to answer. In our case, the answer to *Why?* is that *the truck driver was under the influence of alcohol.* The answer to *Why?* normally requires some discussion in the second and third paragraphs.

HOW?   *How did it happen?* In this case: *The truck driver lost control and drove into the back of the car.*

The hardest part of writing a story is writing the lead. You should therefore make sure that you do not forget to answer the *5Ws and 1H* when you are actually at the scene of your story. Remember these questions when you take notes about what happened and interview bystanders or people who are involved.

Style: developing good lead-writing habits

One problem you are sure to come across is that editors all have their own preferred way of writing a lead. Your newspaper may have a specific house style. If so, become familiar with that style as quickly as possible. However, there are a few rules you can generally apply when you write a lead. The following guidelines also fit in with the basic rules for news writing which are listed on page 108:

1. Make your lead less than 35 words if possible. It can be a bit longer if you need more than one sentence.
2. Make sure you answer the *who, what, where, when, why* and *how* questions if the answers are relevant to the story.
3. Get all information that is basic to the story.
4. Attribute opinion.
5. Always check names, places, dates and times.
6. Don't try to cramp too many words and facts into one sentence.

What do we mean by *attribute opinion*? First, we should decide what is fact and what is opinion. Let's examine the opening sentence of our example lead:

> *CAPE TOWN: A 25-year-old KwaZulu-Natal truck driver, Mr Joe Mkhize, was involved in a collision with a car on the southern bound highway opposite the old power station while under the influence of alcohol.*

How do we know that Joe Mkhize was under the influence of alcohol? Where did we get this information from? Was this just the opinion of the policeman you interviewed, or was Mr Mkhize tested for alcohol? If there is strong evidence that Mr Mkhize was drunk but there is no proof, you must attribute this opinion: that is, you must say whose opinion it was. Here is our lead, rewritten so that the opinion about Mr Mkhize is clearly attributed to the police:

> *CAPE TOWN: A 25-year-old KwaZulu-Natal truck driver, Mr Joe Mkhize, was involved in a collision with a car on the southern bound highway opposite the old power station while allegedly under the influence of liquor. According to police sources at the scene of the accident, Mr Mkhize smelt heavily of liquor and was incoherent.*

As we have said, you should organise your information into *two* lead sentences when necessary. However, because lead sentences do include a lot of information, you may also need to use some conjunctions or linking expressions to help you link up your story smoothly and logically. In journalistic writing it is custom to start sentences with conjunctions such as *and* and *but* although writing purists [those who prefer to keep fixed rules about correct style] may object to it.

Elements that make a good lead

So, what makes a good lead? According to Francois Nel in *Writing for the Media*, the elements that make a good lead are as follows:

- A good lead needs a newsworthy action or result.
- A good lead appeals to a wide readership.
- A good lead gives readers some human interest.
- A good lead gives the reader the most important facts.

Let's look closer at these aspects. Firstly, *a good lead needs a newsworthy action or result*. Basically, the reporter who wishes to write a good lead must remember what news is. (See Chapter 3.) News must be new and it must also be informative, educative and sometimes entertaining. You want people to talk about what they have read, *Wow, Martha, have you heard this?* In other words: *will people be interested in what happened?* Will it affect people's lives? You don't want readers to say, *So what? Who cares a damn?* when they read your lead.

Secondly, *the lead must appeal to a wide readership*, that is to everyone from the professor of nuclear physics to the street sweeper. Thirdly, *there must be some human interest*. A story which deals with strong human emotions and experiences – (e.g. fear, unexpected good fortune, pain, love and romance, anger, reconciliation, death) will appeal to readers. Lastly, *the lead should contain all the important facts*. Although, as we have already pointed out, journalists are always limited by their own picture of the world, every journalist should present the available facts as fully as he/she can.

5 Minute Task

> Check through the final version of the lead paragraph about
> the traffic accident, on page 113. Does it follow all the criteria
> for good lead-writing, and have all the elements of a good
> lead? Support your views.

Different types of leads

There are many different types of leads but we shall limit our discussion to four major types of hard-news leads:

- The *immediate identification* lead.
- The *delayed identification* lead.
- The *summary* lead.
- The *multiple elements* lead.

Conventional hard-news stories normally use a lead which summarises the action in the first few paragraphs.

The immediate identification lead

The main purpose of the *immediate identification* lead is to name the people involved in the story. Why? Usually because the names are more important than the action or event in that particular story. Take for example the following lead:

> *LONDON: Dodi Al Fayed gave Princess Diana a diamond friendship ring worth about R1 million shortly before the car crash that killed them, according to London reports today. (Daily News, 1 September 1997, p1)*

The most significant part of the lead is the personalities involved. There is certainly nothing unusual about rich men giving their women friends expensive diamond rings.

The delayed identification lead

Read this example:

> EAST LONDON: Two German tourists were yesterday
> reported missing in the Transkei region of the Eastern
> Cape. (Daily News, 4 September 1997, p3)

Here the action is more important than the identity of the tourists.
The emphasis is that two foreign tourists have gone missing. Local
people would not recognise their names so their names get sec-
ondary importance.

The summary lead

Where all aspects of the event are important then it is a good idea
to use a summary lead like the following:

> AN ALARMING situation is developing at provincial
> schools, with the chairmen of the governing bodies con-
> sidering handing back power to the government, claim-
> ing they would not be competent without money to run
> schools. (Daily News, 4 September 1997, p3)

The multiple elements lead

The *multiple elements lead* is the most difficult and is used when
one theme for a lead would be too restrictive. The elements are normally introduced in order of perceived importance. Imagine that the
previous example from *The Daily News* had continued as follows:

> AN ALARMING situation is developing at provincial schools,
> with the chairmen of the governing bodies considering
> handing back power to the government, claiming they
> would not be competent without money to run schools.
>
> In a separate incident, school caretakers in the province
> threatened to go on strike if their wage demands of a 15
> percent increase are not met by the government.

In this story, the reporter wants to bring together several local examples of how the budget crisis in education is affecting school governance and management.

5 Minute Task

*At the beginning of this chapter, we mentioned that you would learn how to write a lead in the **inverted pyramid** style. **Inverted** means turned upside down, so that what was at the top is now at the bottom.*

A pyramid is a structure   If you invert it, it
that looks like this.   looks like this.

*Think about this term **inverted pyramid**, and discuss it with a fellow-student if possible. Now that you have read the chapter, why do you think the way of writing a lead that you have been reading about is called the **inverted pyramid** style?*

Conclusion

During this chapter, you have learnt how to construct a lead paragraph, using the inverted pyramid style, as an introduction for a news story. You have learnt what makes a good lead and also how to identify various different types of leads.

Suggested Reading

1. Berry, Thomas Elliot, *Journalism in America,* New York, Hasting House Publishers, 1976.

2. Brooks, Brian S, *et al, The Missouri Group, News Reporting & Writing,* New York, St Martins Press, 4th edition, 1992.

3. Harris, Geoffrey, *Journalism Media Manual – Practical Newspaper Reporting,* 2nd ed, Focal Press, 1993, pp 6-19.

4. Nel, Francois, *Writing for the Media,* Southern Book Publishers, 1994.

5. Teel, Leonard R, *et al, Into the Newsroom – An introduction to journalism,* Prentice-Hall, 1983.

6. Ward, Hiley H, *Professional Newswriting,* New York, Harcourt Brace Jovanovich, Publishers, 1985.

Different styles
10   of writing

Introduction

One of the main problems facing all writers is how to engage people's attention immediately and then how to keep their attention throughout the article. We have to get the story from the page and into our reader's mind. Herbert Spencer summed it up beautifully when he said:

> *"No matter how great the author's wisdom or how vital the message or how remarkable the printer's skill, unread type is merely a lot of paper and a little ink. The true economics of printing must be measured by how much is read and understood and not by how much is produced."* [31.]

How then, do we produce good writing? Good writing has six characteristics:
1. It is precise.
2. It is clear.
3. It has a pace appropriate to the content.
4. It uses transitional devices that lead the reader from one thought to the next.
5. It appeals to the reader's senses.
6. It uses analogies. [32.]

Outcome

In the course of the chapter, we discuss these six characteristics. We shall also look at methods that will show you how to engage your reader's attention. You will learn how not to cram the lead paragraph with too many facts and how to keep the syntax simple and still produce interesting and exciting copy.

By the end of this chapter, you will know more about good writing. You will know how good writing engages the reader's attention and supports his/her understanding. You will know about a variety of writing styles (some tried and tested, and others more recent) that could help you to do this. You will also know about the different kinds of writing found in a newspaper.

5 Minute Task

> Before you read on:
> • Find a newspaper and choose a lead story or long story from the front page.
> • Read about the six characteristics of good writing in the short Introduction to this chapter.
> • Now judge whether the story you have chosen has these six characteristics or not. Pick out examples to support your findings.
> • If you found it difficult to understand and apply any of these criteria, write down your difficulty.
> Now read on.

Six characteristics of good writing

Precision: In good writing, each word is important and words are not wasted. Precision in writing means choosing the exact word for the job. That is why a journalist should never write without a dictionary and a thesaurus. Choose the words you use with precision and care.

Never write *discuss* when you mean *argue* and never use *argue* when you mean *debate* or *dispute*. But these words all mean the same thing, I hear you say. No, they don't. *Discuss* implies a weighing of possibilities by presenting different views. *Argue* implies quite forceful reasoning in support of a conviction that is already held, e.g. *He argued that cinema tickets are too expensive. Debate* suggests formal or public argument between opposing parties or you may debate with yourself whether to do something. *Dispute* implies quarrelsome or heated argument between opposing sides. Of course, you can use any of the above words, but only one is accurate in any particular context.

Sexist language is, of course, offensive, but it is also often *imprecise*. Avoid, if possible, the word *'man'* because most jobs today are carried out by both men and woman, e.g. *'policeman'* should change to *'police officer.'* You can also make your subject plural and so avoid the need to use gender.

Clarity: Before you start to write, think, and then throw out those long complex sentences. Good writing consists mainly of simple sentences with correct grammar and punctuation. In order to achieve this, keep your sentences short. This does not mean that your sentences should be so short that your copy sounds like a machine gun when it is read out loud. Your reader must never be confused about what you are trying to say. After all, the first rule of communication is that the message sent must equal the message received. A good rule is to tell your reader only what he/she needs to know. Don't confuse the reader with superfluous detail.

Plan your story. Ensure that it has a beginning, middle and end. Remember, your lead will dictate the tone and style of the rest of your story so it is important that you take great care with your introduction.

Pace: The length of your sentences usually determines the pace of your story. Pacing is seldom noticed but it is an important technique:

> *"Sentences, as much as the words themselves, give a story mood. Short sentences convey action, tension, movement. A series of long sentences conveys a more relaxed mood; long sentences slow the reader down."* [33.]

Good writers vary the length of their sentences in order to create impact and mood. A short, sharp sentence can change the mood and tone of a story dramatically. Try it.

Transition: *Transition* means to change from one state or condition to another. A good writer uses transitions to lead the reader from one thought to the next. Readers could find any excuse to stop reading at any time; so we use transitions to keep them reading and to allow them no logical place to leave the story until the end.

> *"A transition is a bridge. It can be a word, phrase, a sentence or a paragraph."* [34.] *e.g.: Dave was lost in thought as he waited for the game to begin. His crutches, leaning against the TV, reminded him what might have been. What might have been? Dave was thinking that had he not broken his leg he would have been wearing the green and gold that Saturday.*

The repeated phrase, *What might have been?* is the transition that takes us from Dave's thought to the reason for his not playing.

We can also break a few grammar rules by starting sentences with conjunctions. Your high school grammar teacher would probably frown upon this practice but journalists regularly start sentences with conjunctions like *however, but* and *and.* The practice may not always be strictly correct but it is useful and makes for better reading.

Sensory appeal: It is a journalist's duty to make a story come alive. Who wants to read boring, lifeless copy? But, before we can bring sensory appeal to a story, we must know in detail what happened. *"Information, not language, is the raw material from which effective writing is built."* [35.]

Nel, in *Writing for the Media,* says, *"If a man is shot for playing the same song on the jukebox too many times, I've got to name the tune."* Good writing must appeal to our senses and our sense of curiosity. We must almost be able to see, hear, smell, taste and touch.

Consider the following example from the *Daily News* (Venilla Yoganathan, 5 February 1998, p1).

> *"The controversial Pietermaritzburg-based private medical college has incurred the wrath of a senior national MP who has vowed action at ministerial level.*
>
> *A furious Blade Nzimande, chairman of the central Government's education portfolio committee, yesterday slammed the recently established Edendale College of Medical Sciences as 'bordering on racism and an attempt to recreate apartheid'."*

The truly skilled writer knows when detail really enhances a story. Unnecessary detail may just make it wordy.

5 Minute Task

> Consider Yoganathan's piece with some detail, added as
> follows. Does any of the additional detail improve her story?
> Why/why not?
> The controversial Pietermaritzburg based private medical
> college has incurred the wrath of a senior national MP and
> former political activist, who has vowed action at ministerial
> level. Yesterday, a furious Blade Nzimande, chairman of the
> central Government's education portfolio committee, dressed in
> a green double breasted suit and standing in the blazing sun,
> slammed the recently established Edendale College of
> Medical Sciences as 'bordering on racism and an attempt to
> recreate apartheid'.

Use of analogies: An analogy is a literary device which enables a
writer to show similarities and contrasts. We can do this by using the
words *like* or *as*. Describing how a player had scored a winning
goal, a football writer wrote:

> Having duped the opposition defence, the fans and his
> own management said that he no longer had the pace
> to outrun his markers, he waited until they relaxed and
> he struck like a mamba. That is what he had come for.

In this example, we used a *simile* (*like a mamba*), which compares
one thing to another. *A metaphor*, on the other hand, says one thing
is another, e.g. *His ability to get defences to ignore him makes him
a ghost, when you realise he's there, it's too late.*

What does a good story-teller offer the reader?

Good writing certainly depends partly on clarity, precision, pace,
and using transitions and sensory appeal. But a story won't hold
the reader just by being 'well-dressed' in clear and stylish language.
It also needs good, interesting content as a story. Here are some

qualities you should try to develop in stories you write, if you want the reader to understand and keep reading:

Facts: Facts, not language or style are the foundation from which effective writing is built. If you don't have the facts you cannot write effectively. Too many stories are written instead of being *reported* from a base of solid fact. You can never have too many facts.

Focus: Good stories say one thing. They are clearly focused. They tell about a player rather than the whole match, they do not talk of the economic impact on the country but of the impact on the citizen. These are the stories that endure in the reader's mind.

Faces: People like to read about people. It is the reporter's job to introduce readers to the people who affect and shape their lives in different ways. Readers are affected by laws, trends, scientific discoveries, judicial opinions, etc. These things become more real and immediate to readers when they learn something about the people who are responsible for them. Stories always work best when the reader can 'hear' the opinions, ideas and reactions of people involved in the story.

Form: A good story must have a form that contains and expresses the story. Form allows the story to flow to an inevitable conclusion. Narrative works when the facts are presented to the reader in a chronological form of action and reaction.

Voices:

> "Memorable news stories seem to come from an individual writer speaking aloud to an individual listener. A good newspaper is filled with fascinating conversations. But the writer must remember to keep the voice appropriate to the story .... And we should never forget that even in an age of mass communication the act of reading is private, one writer speaking to one reader." [36.]

Writing styles

Inverted pyramid

In Chapter 8 you learnt how to write in the *inverted pyramid* style. One of the main advantages of the inverted pyramid style of writing is that it is easy to edit. But at the same time this is one of its big disadvantages. We already know that the inverted pyramid delivers the most important news first, and this is the problem. The inverted pyramid does not encourage the reader to read on: there is no real incentive to do so because you already have all the salient facts. Of course, the advantage is that you can skim very quickly through a paper that is written mainly in this style, and that is attractive in our rushed society. But readers are not encouraged to read stories to the end, and the stories lack excitement and suspense. Newspapers written this way are not usually memorable in any way. How, then, can we improve our news writing so that we still give the reader the essential facts but we also keep the story interesting and suspenseful?

Inverted pyramid.

Narrative

A *narrative* is a written or spoken account of connected events in order of happening. The narrative is basic to human experience, it is the way we explain our situation to one another. In newspapers, the narrative is the mother of all forms of writing. Here are some pointers about writing narrative:

- The best way to start a narrative is with a *character*. As we have already said, people like to read about people. Report what characters do and how they do it. In this way the characters reveal themselves to us and our readers. *Conflict* (that is, the clash between characters) is central to a story. Use characters and their interaction to move your story forward.

- Use *dialogue* – let your characters speak to one another and your readers. Reveal your characters' thoughts through internal dialogue.

- Show the reader the world or place where the action takes place.

- Narratives are best told in the third person: that is *he* or *she* or *Cynthia* or *Mr Gumede*. Readers identify most easily with third person characters.

- Do not end your story with a conclusion that tells the reader what to think. It is too late for that. You should end with an *action* that allows the reader to come to their own conclusion.

Wall Street Journal

The *focus structure* of writing is certainly not a new or original style of writing, but it is a very successful style that was successfully adopted by one of the world's great newspapers, the *Wall Street Journal*.

The focus style uses the device of focusing on an individual or institution before moving on to report on the larger, more important, issue. The writer then provides a strong finish that often returns to the original subject of the focus.

Consider the following example by Wonder Hlongwa entitled, *Cause of death: staff shortages* (*Mail & Guardian*, 6 to 12 February 1998, p14):

   1.   *Thandeka Shabalala (16) lies on a stretcher at the King Edward VIII Hospital in Durban, with a heavy brown blanket thrown over her body despite the heat.*

2. She has travelled all the way from Pietermaritzburg.
    She is one of the hundreds of patients who come for
    treatment at King Edward and instead either sleep
    on stretchers for a couple of nights or leave untreated.

3. The hospital has severe shortages of nursing staff,
    general assistants and messengers. But it has to cope
    with an influx of thousands of patients from different
    corners of the country's most populated province.

4. Over the past two years at least 10 people have
    died at King Edward because of staff shortages.

5. Senior nurses complain they have only half the staff
    they need to perform their duties effectively. They
    are ignoring a call by the government to volunteer
    an extra two hours a day in an attempt to treat all
    the people who come seeking help.

6. Nurses say they already 'slave' the entire working
    day because of the overwhelmingly high nurse-
    patient ratio.

7. "Our worker's forum wrote a number of letters to
    the chief medical superintendent asking for a
    change in the admission system. We even sent them
    statistics on a daily basis, detailing patients who
    have spent more than one night but who have not
    received treatment, and those who died on
    stretchers," said a nursing sister.

8. The outpatients' department is the most crowded
    at King Edward, with more than 500 patients on a
    daily basis. The dispensary has no seats for patients
    waiting for their medicines. Some lean against the
    wall, while others wait in passages nearby.

9. The overcrowding is not only caused by patients with
    serious ailments who require treatment at a central
    hospital like King Edward. Hundreds come from the
    surrounding townships with minor ailments that can

> *be treated in a local clinic. They have their reasons for shunning the clinics.*
>
> 10. *"My child can't eat, he's got diarrhoea and sores next to his penis. I'm from Umlazi township, we have a clinic nearby but it doesn't have medication," said Pretty-Girl Zulu, mother of seven month-old Memory.*
>
> 11. *Because of a shortage of hospital porters, patients have to be carried into the hospital by their relatives. And because of the shortage of stretchers and wheel-chairs, a patient was seen being brought into the hospital in a supermarket trolley.*

Hlongwa has used the method well. In the first two paragraphs he focuses on an individual, Thandeka the young patient. Midway through paragraph two, Hlongwa transcends to the larger issue, King Edward's severe staff shortages. He then continues to report on the larger issue through paragraphs three to nine. In paragraph 10 he returns to a 'close-up' individual focus. In this case he uses the mother of an infant patient. He concludes his article with a strong finish, to tie the whole article together.

You will notice that the body of Hlongwa's story is constructed in the same manner as the inverted pyramid method. Thus, when you use this method you must remember that after your introduction you should arrange your facts in descending order of importance. Your ability to maintain your reader's interest will depend on your writing skills. Remember, practice makes perfect.

The *focus* of your story is very important and if you do not choose your focus carefully and introduce your focus skilfully you will lose your reader. Nearly any story can be written this way but you must have focus, detail and transitions.

It is important to have a strong finish, and a good technique is to return to the original focus that you introduced at the beginning or like Hlongwa, to bring in another strong detail like the supermarket trolley.

Some new writing styles

Champagne glass

This style takes a similar form to the inverted pyramid, with the top/first half of the story containing a strong lead and all the important facts. From the important facts there is a strong transition to a chronological retelling of the story from beginning to end. This style of story should end with a great kicker. It is important to give your readers a 'reward' for staying with you for the whole story. According to Don Fry of the Poynter Institute, the great thing about this style of writing is that it simplifies complex events by retelling them in narrative order and it keeps the story in context. The only problem though, according to Fry, is that this kind of story is much harder to edit.

Anecdote and nut graph

This style has the advantage (according to Don Fry) that it can lead the reader easily into difficult subjects and complex analyses. This happens because stories written in this style start with a long, soft lead. This could be an interesting description or anecdote [a short and striking story] which is linked to the hard news in the story, but does not contain the core facts. The hard news appears only in the paragraph following the lead, and then the rest of the story follows.

The paragraph following the soft lead is called the 'nut graph'. The 'nut graph' tells the reader what the story is all about, i.e. it gives the essential facts which show why the story is so important.

Stack of blocks

This style takes the form of a lead followed by several distinct and separate sections and a strong ending. The advantage of grouping information into specific sections is that it allows for easier explanation and helps readers remember the major points. The major disadvantage is that a reader has to scan an entire story to get all the points. The style does make editing easier because whole sections of the story that are less important can be removed without the rest of the story being affected.

10 Minute Task

> Find several different newspapers, including both weekly and
> daily newspapers aimed at different readers.
> * Note down the different writing styles you can find in
>   different stories.
> * Do particular newspapers seem to use certain styles more
>   than other newspapers do?
> * Are particular styles more common in certain sections of
>   newspapers than in other sections?
> This task will take you longer than 10 minutes if you do it thor-
> oughly, but you will probably find this to be worth your while.

Different applications of news writing

News story

There is no doubt that the basis of all news writing is the news story.
What is news? Chapter 3 offers some answers to this question, as
you will probably remember. Of course you may, like many reporters,
find that *"news is pretty much whatever your editor decides it is"*. [37.]
But by now you know that news must be timely, new and interesting
to the public. News reporters must constantly improve their news-
gathering skills so that they can present stories that make readers
look keenly for the next edition.

The news story demands accurate story telling under great pressure
and in a limited time. Because of this pressure on the writing and
editing of news stories, most editors prefer to keep to the *inverted
pyramid* style of writing. Why? The formula is simple in structure and
allows for simple editing. It has been tried and tested and found
reliable.

Of course not all news stories are the same, and some require more
journalistic skill than others. Reports on deaths, accidents and crime,
for example, do not generally require the reporter to 'read' and
interpret the facts skilfully. However, reporting on courts, trials, lawsuits, politics, business, education, science or religion requires the

reporter to have some specialist knowledge and skills. Similarly, reporting on entertainment, theatre, films, books, sport, and lifestyle could require the reporter to have a variety of skills and knowledge. Whenever a story requires a reporter to *interpret* and *investigate* (i.e. to look beneath the obvious facts and events), that story will challenge the reporter's skills and knowledge.

Feature story/columns

It is the job of the feature story to put the news into perspective. The feature story fills in the *human interest* factor that time and space do not allow for in the news story. Feature stories used to be called 'human interest' stories. Feature stories usually give the journalist more opportunity to experiment with angles [different approaches to the story] and with language. People love to read about people and that is why we have different types of feature story such as the *profile* [a detailed look at a well-known personality] and *trend stories* about the latest fashions in lifestyle, clothing, music, etc.

Analysis story

The analysis or interpretive story is often referred to as a *think piece.* We are normally drowned in this type of story when the minister of finance gives his annual budget speech in the middle of March. Just about every part of his speech is subjected to analysis in order to make his message clearer to the general public. Some might say that the message is usually very clear for example, *you are going to pay more taxes and get less in return.*

Clarity of writing is essential when dealing with an interpretive piece because generally the subject would not need interpreting if it were clear in the first place. The idea is to help your readers understand and learn.

Investigative story

Budding investigative journalists should heed the words of the late Chris Hani, politician and former SACP general secretary, *"Don't trust the politicians. I should know – I am one myself."* **38.**

Lord Deedes, a British politician and editor, brought the role of the investigative journalist into focus when he said, *"Politicians will never admit to anything disadvantageous to themselves, and it is the duty of newspapers to tell people when a politician wishes to remain silent."* **39.**

Probably more young journalists are drawn to journalism through the heroic deeds of investigative reporters than any other form of reporting. However, investigative reporting demands extremely careful preparation and research. The investigative reporter is strongly accountable to the reader. These things make investigative reporting a really tough job that suits only the most diligent [careful and hard-working] reporter.

Some key points about investigative reporting (also see Chapter 13): Before you write about a person or an institution in a negative way, it is important to ensure that all your facts are irrefutable [that they can be proved to be true]. If you don't, you are liable to be sued in court for libel.

One of your most important acts when preparing for an interview is the phrasing of your questions. How you structure your questions often determines whether or not you get the answer you were looking for.

In your writing, it is important that you show unequivocally [so that there can be no doubt] that your story is fair and that you cannot be accused of acting unethically. Only reveal a fact after it has been verified and is unassailable [no-one can contradict or deny it].

Editorials

Editorials are the one area where the writer is allowed to be biased, one-sided, opinionated and subjective. As a young journalist, it is unlikely that you will get the opportunity to write an editorial for many years. The editorial pages are usually quite distinct from the rest of the paper. Only here do newspapers demand the opinion of the writer. Editorials are usually written by the editor or by an invited person.

There are a number of different types of editorial: the *unsigned editorial* which often reflects the opinions of an editorial board; the *editorial column* with bylines and mugshots of the author; and *letters* to the editor which give readers the chance to air their views.

Reviews

Each reviewer is loved by some and hated by others. The reason for this is simple, we each have our own opinion. You know what happens when you go to a movie and thoroughly enjoy it only to read that the critics hated it. You are outraged, how dare the reviewer write such nonsense about the movie?

On the other hand, perhaps you have often gone to a show that you considered appalling, yet it received rave reviews. Most newspapers have their reviewers who write for them on specialist areas such as music, art, theatre and dance. Reviewers are usually more merciful than *critics*, who are usually experts in their respective fields.

Sports writing

Many people see sports writing as a form of writing all on its own, but this impression is not correct. Sports writing is simply a combination of news and feature writing about sport. Sports stories are essentially action stories which contain all the elements of a good story: passion, courage, triumph, heartbreak, love and hate.

Consider this great quote from sports journalist Jon Swift: *"In the overall context of sport and life, victory is far more important than Baron de Coubertin's dictum that taking part is good enough."* [40.] Where else would you get a quote like that than on the sports pages?

Because of the complexities of today's sport, sports writers have to have an understanding of many subjects such as finance, law, sponsorships and even medicine and health issues.

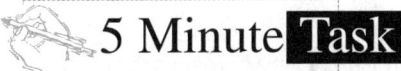

5 Minute Task

> - Look through the information in the last few pages about different applications of writing. Decide which kinds of stories you think you would most enjoy writing and why.
> - Then look through the section on different writing styles and select those styles which you think would be most appropriate for the kinds of stories you would prefer to write.
> - You will find it useful to go further than this and practise re-writing newspaper stories in another style, or writing new stories of your own in a variety of styles.

Conclusion

In this chapter, you have learnt how to engage people's attention immediately and then how to maintain their attention throughout the article. You have learnt how to get the story from the page, into the reader's mind, and how to produce good writing.

Do not forget the six characteristics of good writing: precision, clarity, pace, transitions, analogies and the appeal to the readers' senses. In addition you should now know something about different writing styles, i.e. different ways of organising stories.

Finally, you have learnt about the different kinds of writing that are found in a newspaper. If you work at your writing you will soon be able to engage your readers' attention and produce interesting and exciting copy in a variety of writing styles. Over time, you will become skilled at writing for different sections of a publication.

Suggested Reading

1. Berry, Thomas Elliot, *Journalism in America*, New York, Hasting House Publishers, 1976.

2. Brooks, Brian S, *et al*, The Missouri Group, *News Reporting & Writing*, New York, St Martins Press, 4th edition, 1992.

3. Harris, Geoffrey, *Journalism Media Manual – Practical Newspaper Reporting*, 2nd ed, Focal Press, 1993.

4. Nel, Francois, *Writing for the Media*, Southern Book Publishers, 1994.

5. Teel, Leonard R, *et al*, *Into the Newsroom – An introduction to journalism*, Prentice-Hall, 1983.

6. Ward, Hiley H, *Professional Newswriting*, New York, Harcourt Brace Jovanovich Publishers, 1985.

Editing –

11 getting it right

Introduction

Editor is a term which has various meanings in newspaper and other media settings. You need to understand the difference between the person who is the editor of the newspaper and the sub- or copy-editors who edit stories before publication.

Firstly, the editor is the head of a newspaper's staff and is the link between the journalist staff and the board of directors of that newspaper. The editor must decide on the policy of the newspaper and make sure that staff work accordingly. The editor is finally accountable for the success or failure of the newspaper. A fitting sign for an editor's desk is one that says, *The Buck Stops Here* [in other words: *I am the person who is finally accountable*].

Editors are therefore often autocratic [dominating] leaders who stamp their personality and will on their newspapers. Editors usually exert their influence by writing the editorial comment and controlling the editorial pages. You as a reporter will have little or no contact with the editor unless you work for a small community newspaper. You will feel the editor's influence through those who report directly to the editor like the news editor and the assistant editors. This influence is usually applied during the editors' conference where the different editors plan what will go into an issue.

However, this chapter does not really deal with the work of the actual editor of the newspaper. It focuses more on the editing that happens when sub-editors prepare a written story for publication. The sub-editors (also called *copy-editors*) do apply the editorial policy of their own newspaper when they edit stories. But they also use some more general principles of newspaper writing and editing, that is, principles that are similar from newspaper to newspaper.

Outcome

At the end of this chapter, you should know what copy-editors or sub-editors do. You should understand how to edit copy as well as the principles of writing and designing headlines.

5 Minute Task

> Before you read on:
> By now you know that sub- or copy-editors prepare the stories
> that reporters have already written for publication.
> * Think about the different steps the reporter has taken with
>   the story by the time it reaches the sub-editor, i.e. following
>   leads from contacts or tip-offs, doing research, conducting
>   interviews, writing up the story and the lead for the story, etc.
> * Consider what might need to be done to the story before it
>   can be printed. Brainstorm your ideas with a partner if
>   possible, and list them. Write down anything you can think of.
> Now read on.

What is copy editing?

Copy editing or sub-editing is the assembling, preparing, modifying
and condensing of written material for publication, that is, putting
the material together, correcting or altering it, making it shorter
where necessary, etc.

It is the copy-editor or sub-editor's duty to
* make the story readable.
* keep the story brief and to the point.
* guard against libel.
* check the accuracy of the story.
* make sure the story fits the newspaper's tone and style.

A copy-editor could alter a story by
* increasing or decreasing the text.
* rewording (this is where your thesaurus comes in handy).
* correcting and changing what is emphasised in the story.
* checking verifiable facts [things that can be proved correct or
  incorrect], including the correct spelling of names and
  addresses.
* composing headlines.

Copy editing is one of the most important functions in the newspaper or magazine newsroom. The copy/sub-editor must make the story readable and ensure that it fits the requirements of journalistic writing. Phrases must not be ambiguous [have more than one possible meaning] and the writing must be clear, forceful and easy to understand at the first reading. This is difficult to achieve because newspaper readers represent a wide range of education from those who are newly literate to university graduates. The copy must be understood by all without offending any. The sub-editor must find the acceptable 'middle road'.

Efficient and accurate copy editing is taken for granted by readers, in fact they don't notice it. But bad copy editing can make or break a newspaper's hard earned reputation. Readers always remember the mistakes and therefore sub-editors are the publication's last defence against errors.

What skills should a sub-editor possess? An important skill is *a sound knowledge of the specific meaning of words*. Moreover, sub-editors should be experienced reporters who are well-informed, confident and skilled in the use of language. Sadly, modern newsrooms do not always observe all these requirements, and their publications lose quality as a result.

The sub-editor must *enforce deadlines* so that the newspaper is produced on time. Sub-editors often have to work extremely fast to meet those deadlines. As you can imagine, the job does not suit the inexperienced. As a reporter, you will have little contact with the sub-editors unless they wish to query aspects of your article.

Since most newspapers today are produced using desk top publishing (DTP), sub-editors are responsible for the copy editing as well as the layout and design of the pages.

How to edit copy

First do nothing. The best way to start editing a story is to do nothing to the story except read through it at least twice. Only then, after reading the story for the second time and getting a sense of what the writer is trying to say, should you begin to edit.

A golden rule (which many sub-editors unfortunately ignore) *is not to make any changes to the style and content of a story without consulting the writer.* I paid dearly for ignoring this rule. When I was editor of a national sports publication, I employed a well known writer to write a column for me. The writer used to submit her articles to me on a stiffy disc, so when I received her article I put the article through a spell check without first reading the story. The very last word had been incorrectly spelt so I corrected it, still without reading the piece. The story was duly published and I soon had the writer on the phone shouting that the misspelt word was the punchline of the story.

Ask: *does the story make sense?* What point is the writer making? Is that point made clearly? Is there sufficient information to support that point of the story? Is the information arranged in a logical order? Are the arguments well balanced, and is opinion clearly distinguished from fact?

Ask: *what (if anything) in the story could be cut?* Some stories benefit from cutting because they are too long, with parts that reduce the strong thrust of the story. Others have to be cut simply because there is a shortage of space on the page. If you must cut, make sure that your cuts do not destroy the sense of the story.

Ask: *is there any information that should be checked for accuracy?* There may be information in the story that, if inaccurate, could involve your publication in great trouble and expense. Check this information with the writer if this has not already been clarified, or do the necessary reference and telephone work.

Ask: *does the style of the story involve the reader and fit the publication?* The story may make sense but this is not enough. It is important that the story involve the reader. The style of the writing should be appropriate for the intended medium and audience.

Check grammar and spelling. Is the story easy to read? Are sentences concise, clear, and written in the active voice? Has a grammar and spelling check been carried out?

Guard against libel. Eliminate or rewrite any statement that may libel the subject. Defence against libel is difficult so it is important that you take care when using words like *liar, drunk, cheat,* etc.

10 Minute Task

- *Find two or three news pages from any recent daily newspaper.*
- *Select three or four stories from those pages.*
- *Apply the guidelines for sub-editing to these stories and decide whether the sub-editors have done a good job in each case or not. Give your reasons for judging as you do.*

Headlines

The term *headline* means the words above a story which show what it is about. Writing headlines is one of the most difficult sub-editing tasks. You could even say that headline writing is an art. You can follow certain rules, but, like all arts, headline writing cannot just be reduced to a simple formula.

It is the headline that is the window to the story and convinces the reader to read on. Even an excellent story is useless if it is not read. But it is not easy to write inviting, convincing headlines, as one writer puts it:

> *"Choosing the right words is difficult, and the headline writer's job is further complicated by space and design requirements. Sometimes there is only enough space for two or three words to a line, or maybe half a dozen words for headlines that are stacked several columns deep."* [41.]

What are the functions of a headline?

To summarise the story for the reader: Most readers scan a newspaper and only read articles which interest them. The headline therefore serves to summarise the story and arouse the reader's attention enough for him/her to begin reading the story.

To attract the reader's attention: Many newspapers are sold and read because someone has been attracted by a headline. Headlines of feature stories can be humorous or thought-provoking, but headlines for straight news stories are mostly quite direct and conventional.

To show how important the story is: The larger the headline, the more important the reader will expect the story to be. The size of a headline should therefore be related to the importance of the story during copy editing. If a story has a large, bold headline, the editor is expecting the story to be read thoroughly.

To give prominence to the newspaper: Well-written headlines improve the look of a newspaper and give it impact over its competitors. Good headlines break the monotony of looking at columns and columns of grey type. It is for this reason that most newspapers try to adopt a distinctive [special] look and design for their headlines.

How to write headlines

Here are the basic general guidelines that you should use for writing headlines:

Summarise: A good sub-editor must have the ability to summarise a story effectively. The headline of a news story is often a summary of the lead paragraph.

Check readability: A headline *must* be intelligible and understood at the first reading. Always ask yourself the question: *Does this headline make sense?* A good headline should also look attractive and uncluttered.

Develop a good command of vocabulary. In order to write good headlines, you must develop un extensive vocabulary and be able to use words that create interest, summarise the story and arouse your readers' curiosity. A good headline creates imagery, e.g. 'Romeo' for a lover, 'Cop' for police officer. Also, you will need to be able to produce synonyms easily so that you can find simple, clear words for headlines (see next page).

Here are some more specific rules about how to use language in headlines.

Use synonyms:

You will need these especially to substitute short words for long ones, e.g.
>   *job, career* or *work* for *employment;*
>   *test* or *probe* for *examination;*
>   *make* or *build* for *manufacture.*
It is essential to have a good thesaurus handy so that you can choose the correct synonym.

For stronger impact use the active voice:

Poor: Students warned by SRC President (passive voice)
Better: SRC President warns students

Use specific language:

Poor: Player hurt in soccer match
Better: Player breaks leg in soccer tackle

Avoid using ambiguous or confusing language:

Poor: Strikers ignore salary plans from management
Better: Strikers ignore management's salary plans

Feature stories should have appropriate headlines:

Poor: Fraudsters rob Children's Fund
Better: Children fund fraudsters

Include a verb so that the headline does not appear as a label:

Poor: Rain storm
Better: Rain storm causes damage

Attribute opinion in headlines:

Poor: Students warned
Better: SRC President warns students

Designing headlines

When writing headlines, you also need to consider visual design and space requirements. The designer has to choose whether to use all caps or caps and lower case. All caps headlines are difficult to read and are not often used.

STUDENT LEADERS MEET MANDELA

The standard style is to capitalise the first letter of each word and in the contemporary choice only the first word and proper names are capitalised.

Student Leaders Meet Mandela
(Standard style)

Student leaders meet Mandela
(Contemporary style)

Most headlines are simply one line and set flush left.

10 Minute Task

> *Find some recent daily or weekly newspapers. Work with a partner if possible.*
> * *Cut out four stories (two from the news pages and two from the feature pages). Cut off their headlines and give the stories to your partner without the headlines. Your partner should do the same for you. (If you are working alone, try not to look at the headlines before you cut – you could try folding them back quickly.)*
> * *Try to write headlines for the four stories. Apply all the guidelines for writing and designing headlines in this chapter.*
> * *Now compare your headlines with the original headlines in the newspaper. Decide whether yours are more effective or less effective than the original headlines and why. If you are working with a partner, discuss this together.*

Conclusion

In this chapter, you learnt what copy-editors or sub-editors do. You learnt how to edit copy as well as the principles of writing and designing headlines.

Suggested Reading

1. Berry, Thomas Elliot, *Journalism in America,* New York, Hasting House Publishers, 1976.

2. Brooks, Brian S, *et al, The Missouri Group, News Reporting & Writing,* New York, St Martins Press, 5th edition, 1992.

3. Harriss, Julian, *et al, The Complete Reporter,* New York, Macmillan Publishing Co., Inc., 4th edition, 1981.

4.   Hodgson, F W, *Journalism Media Manual – Subediting,* Focal
      Press, 1993.

5.   Nel, Francois, *Writing for the Media,* Southern Book Publishers,
      1995.

6.   Oosthuizen, Lucas M, *Introduction to Communication –
      Course book 5: journalism, press and radio studies,* Cape
      Town, Juta & Co. Ltd., 1996.

The beat –
12   different areas of reporting

Introduction

M any, many articles are needed to fill a newspaper every day. It takes much planning and organisation to control the large number of reporters who work on each edition of a newspaper. The newspaper generally divides its reporters into *beat* reporters, *general assignment* reporters and *special assignment* reporters. Writing style may need to be a bit different from one beat to another. But although one aspect of writing may be emphasised for one beat, this does not mean that it has no relevance for the other beats. In this chapter, we will examine the different kinds of reporters' roles.

Outcome

At the end of this chapter, you will understand the role of both the general assignment and the beat reporter. You will also understand the special requirements and demands of the work on different beats and what special skills you will require to cover a specific beat.

Covering a beat

Beat reporting is the foundation of a newspaper's news coverage. Reporters on the different beats keep their readers informed about what is happening on their beats. Beats cover various topics such as crime, the courts, local government, national government, business, sport, education, entertainment, art, health, environment, etc., to name but a few. Today, assignments are made more on the basis of issues than on specific topics. Also, it is difficult to stick exclusively to one beat when reporting. For example, a story on the environment may touch not only on crime, but also on local government, government, business, education and health. Social issues such as the plight of street children may touch on all the same topics as well as welfare, employment, and tourism. So, while a story might start in a particular beat, beat reporting should not exclude other topics.

5 Minute Task

> Before you read on:
> • What kind of approach and behaviour do you think is most
>   important for the reporter who has to cover a beat (any beat)?
> • List some of these qualities and briefly note your reasons for
>   each one.
> Now read on.

Whatever beat you cover, there are a few basic principles that you should stick to if you want to be successful 'on the beat'.

Be prepared: Information is power. Get to know your beat and the people in it. If you are new on the beat, read a lot of past reports relating to that beat. This research is almost the same as the preparation required for an interview but more detailed, since it covers many different stories and aspects from the past. Memorise the names that seem to appear again and again. Ask for advice from reporters who have previously worked that beat. Above all, try not to go in blind – forewarned is forearmed.

Talk to sources: Once you have read as widely as possible, it is time to start talking to people. Ask your predecessor which sources have been the most reliable ones up to now. Who can you trust and who will lie to you? Get as much background information as you can on these sources. Treat all information given to you with caution. Be sceptical – journalists, even those leaving a beat, do not like giving away hard earned sources to other journalists.

Once you have all the background information available, you are ready to start covering your beat. In the first few weeks on the beat, try to meet as many of the important role-players as possible. Remember, it is just as important for your new sources to get to know you as it is for you to get to know them, because at this point you are trying to establish a relationship. If you are well-prepared, you are less likely to ask silly questions and you will have a better chance of establishing a *rapport* [a successful and two-sided communication] with your source.

Be alert: Important stories do not come with flags and bells attached. Sometimes, even the people involved don't realise that the story is significant and/or relevant for the public. Always ask yourself the following questions:

1. Is this important?
2. Who could gain from this and who could lose?
3. How much will this cost and who will pay?

When you have the answers to these questions, you may find that your story is much bigger than you realised.

Be persistent: Don't give up! Ask the question(s) you need to ask. It is what you are trained for, what you are paid for and what you owe your readers. Do not ask your next question until you have received a satisfactory answer to your first question. Keep your source on the subject and don't let them lead you off the topic – a favourite ploy [trick] of politicians who are well-known for not answering questions directly. Remember the interviewing techniques you learnt in Chapter 7. Always ask yourself, *Does this make sense to me?* and do not quit until it does. If it doesn't make sense to you, it will not make sense to your readers.

Keep a file or a diary of events that you can follow up. Remember some situations or events take many months to develop so it is important to diarise any events that relate to the main developing story. This will remind you to check on progress.

Make contact: There is no substitute for personal contact. *For the beat reporter, the telephone just does not work* and the only way to cover the beat is to be there. It is important for you to become part of the community you are trying to cover. Remember the golden rule of being nice to people? This is doubly important when you cover a beat. You need the help and goodwill of many people such as clerks, secretaries and drivers.

Protect your sources: Not only is this basic to good journalism, not only is it unethical to reveal your sources, but you will also find that many people will only talk to you if they are kept anonymous. Once you agree not to disclose your source, you are bound to that promise.

Be accurate: There is no quicker way to lose the respect of the people on your beat than through inaccurate reporting. Check and double check your facts. If you are not certain of something, do not publish it.

Do a favour: As a reporter you will spend a lot of your time asking people for favours such as giving you information they need not share. If asked for a favour, and it is possible to do it, do so. You will earn valuable goodwill.

Be vigilant [watchful and cautious]: Do not forget that your job is to keep your readers properly informed. All the effort you put in to covering your beat is for one purpose only and to lose sight of that purpose is to lose sight of your job. Remember that sources can control reporters but reporters can't control sources. Before you react to information by reporting it, try to clarify *why* your source is giving you certain information. You must be quite sure that you have not been manipulated by your source into accepting a biased view. Of course you won't be able to stop this from happening now and then. But be wary for the sake of your reputation and for your readers.

10 Minute Task

Before you read on:
Consider the four main areas of beat reporting: court reporting, local government/municipal reporting, sports reporting and business reporting. For each of these, decide:
* *What would be your main objective for this kind of reporting?*
* *What would be your main problems in this kind of reporting?*
* *What kind of writing style would be suitable for this kind of reporting, for most newspapers?*
Jot down a few notes on each point, then read on.

Court reporting

Because of the present state of the criminal justice system, court reporting is not the easiest beat a reporter can be assigned to. Court reporters spend more time in the clerk of the court's office than in the proper courts. However, court reporting is always one beat that is demanded by readers. The public want to know who is passing through the courts and why.

It is impossible to cover every case that comes before the courts so it is very important to *select trials carefully*. Court stories can be the most difficult and demanding to get and to write because legal issues and arguments are complex and often difficult to follow and explain to others. Yet strict accuracy in reporting is obviously important whether the information is collected inside or outside the court. An added problem a reporter has to face when publishing court stories is how much the publicity will affect the court's decision. There are a few rules to bear in mind when covering the courts.

Never trust a lawyer's word: Lawyers must make sure that their clients get as little negative publicity as possible, in fact, they will often try to reflect bad publicity onto someone else. You should interpret everything a lawyer says as trying to defend the lawyer's client. In other words, don't take a lawyer as an objective and an unbiased source. Lawyers will do their best to use the press to gain some advantage for their clients.

Truth and justice do not always win: Both the defence and the prosecution conceal evidence that they think is prejudicial to their case [evidence that could weaken their case]. Defence lawyers will use technicalities to free their clients and judges may misinterpret or ignore rules. It is a sad fact of life that innocent people do sometimes go to jail and guilty ones go free.

A reporter's major source in court cases is the *court record*. This is the official transcript of the case. However, readers want more than the court record, so it is important to cultivate sources like clerks, translators, lawyers and police officers who can help you describe the court action more fully.

Local government reporting

Politicians, even minor local government politicians, cannot survive without the help of the press. Politicians need a platform to address their constituencies and the press is that platform. One of the fundamentals of a democracy and a free society is a free press. The press plays a major role in supplying the public with information about government. There have been governments and politicians who have tried to subvert [put down, discredit] the press. Two good examples of this are the *'Info scandal'* or *'Muldergate'* in South Africa and the *'Watergate scandal'* in the USA in the 1970s. The only way to prevent such scandals is to ensure the press have direct access to all public records. Government is public business and it is the public's right to know what their government is doing on their behalf. Councillors and public officials are often in conflict with the press but most recognise that government needs the press to govern effectively and to show the people that democracy is at work.

When assigned to cover local government, a journalist should immediately find out which people are the power centres who influence the flow of money to various competing projects. Politics, even local government politics, is all about how money and power get distributed.

Who are the main players and sources in local government? Obviously, *the mayor* is a major source, and so are council members, council officials, pressure groups, business groups and political opponents. Don't forget that members of the public are role-players and sources too.

How can the journalist help readers to make sense of what goes on in local government? The most important rule is to *write and translate for your readers*. Politicians and bureaucrats tend to use jargon that the public doesn't understand, so the journalist must learn how to translate this jargon into standard English. Make your writing come alive. Tell your readers how it will affect their lives if a certain bill, act, resolution or decision is put into force. For example, if displaced people are to be moved off the land they are squatting on, where will they move to? Has new housing been allocated to them? Who will move them? The public also need to know the cost of council decisions on their pockets. If councillors are seeking a salary increase what will that increase cost each citizen? Go and see what is happening. If you think that the public transport is inefficient, use it and discover for yourself how its inefficiency impacts on Joe Public. Always make sure that you have answered all the questions your reader will ask, and above all do not forget the 5Ws + 1H (see Chapter 9).

Sports reporting

Interest in sport remains high but much sport reporting today is weak. Sports writers seem to be unaware that with the ball-by-ball commentaries and TV, *readers usually already know and have seen what happened* and do not need the writer to repeat it. Rather, *they want to know the story behind the story.* Leonard Schecter was harsh when he characterised most sports reporters as "*so droolingly grateful for the opportunity to make their living as non-paying fans at sporting events that they devoted much of their energy to stepping on no toes.".42.* We do have a number of fine sports journalists who know a lot and are respected by administrators, fans and players alike, but they are few and far between. Many sports journalists seem to feel that they alone can give unjustified and unresearched opinions – opinions which are followed by a well-rehearsed silence when they are proven wrong.

As in all forms of beat reporting, it is important in sports reporting to *be prepared.* The preparation is the same as for any other beat. Sport tends to bring out the best and worst in people so it is essential to understand the psychology of the sport you are reporting on. What qualities do particular sports require of the sportsperson? You also need to understand the history and sociology involved. Sport played a major role in the struggle for freedom in South Africa and the history affects sport today. Apartheid is directly responsible for the fact that there are so few blacks that have made an impact in sports such as cricket, rugby, swimming and golf.

In sport reporting, *sources* are just as important as they are in other forms of reporting: players, former players, coaches, managers, administrators, sponsors, spouses, etc. can all offer important information and background knowledge.

In many cases, readers will turn to the sport pages first when they read a newspaper. *If readers give that much importance to the sport page, it should carry writing and reporting of the highest standard.* The quality of the sports page can make or break a newspaper. *Sports writers therefore need a detailed knowledge of all aspects of the games or sports that they write about.* Although a sports writers do not need to have played a sport especially well themselves, it obviously helps if they have. And it certainly helps if they are really enthusiastic about the sport they are covering. Horse-racing writers tend to be enthusiasts who are totally involved in their chosen sport.

A great difficulty for sports reporters (much more than for political or crime reporting) is *keeping a critical distance from the beat.* Part of the reason for this is that most sports writers become sports writers because they are passionate about sport or about a particular sport. It is hard for sports writers to hide their bias and to separate themselves from their links and affiliations. A few years ago, *Manning Rangers* were leading the *South African Premier Soccer* league by many points and with only a mathematical chance of being overtaken by their nearest rivals. On a lunch-time talk show on radio *SAFM* just before the end of the season, local sports writers and commentators discussed how Manning Rangers were going to be pipped at the post. In their minds, the unsung Durban team could never, never win the league. Yet every bit of logical evidence showed clearly that they would.

Good sports writing will be vigorous, virile and exciting but not so exaggerated that it is not believable. Sports writing does at times stretch the boundaries of standard English, and the sports writer must find his/her own style. This does not mean the sports writer can forget the basic rules of good grammar. It does mean that because sports writers are usually given a bit more freedom of style, they should have an especially good command of language. A good sports writer brings the event to the people with all the excitement and emotion that spectators and contestants felt when it happened. The informality of writing used on most sports pages permits the sports reporter to use colloquialisms, metaphors, similes and other figures of speech which other reporters avoid.

Always remember that although you are writing for your readers and the fans, *the coaches, the managers and the players will also read your story.* If your story is not accurate and fair you will lose their respect and goodwill. These are essential for your success on the sports beat.

How to write a good sports story

One of the most important and difficult parts of a sports writer's job is *covering contests, games and matches.* Sports writers must make all the normal writing decisions about angle, lead, quotes, etc. that other journalists must make. But, as I have already pointed out, they also have to deal with the fact that most readers already know a lot about the event and many were there, or listened on radio or watched on TV. They already know what happened and expect you to tell them the *how* and *why.* This all has to happen very quickly because sports reporters normally have very tight deadlines.

It is essential that sports writers add value to their reports. You can build that value through research before the match, for example, you can find out about players carrying an injury into the match. You must get the story behind the story. Get the human interest angle, make your readers feel that they are part of the build-up to the match and when you write about the match make them feel that they are part of the action. Find out what made this event different, what was unique [special] about it. Do not forget to tell the reader who won and describe the action. But also ask yourself what the reader wants to know, and answer those questions. Above all, get the players and coaches into your story by using good quotes.

Do not forget the six characteristics of good writing we dealt with in Chapter 10: that is, *precision, clarity, pace, transitions, sensory appeal* and the *use of analogies*. Also, remember what helps a reader understand a story, i.e. *facts, focus, faces, form* and *voices*.

Business reporting

Business news, both local and international, forms a major part of any newspaper. The increased importance of the economy has brought a demand for reporters who have training in economics and finance as well as journalism. Today, business is big news and newspapers have expanded both the quantity and quality of their coverage of commerce and industry.

The style of business reporting has also changed. Business pages are filled with investigative and analytical stories, profiles on corporate decision-makers and stories on how business is benefiting the community. Quite often a story with a business or economic angle is the lead story of the day and just about any story can have an economic or business angle. For example, a story about teachers who lack the necessary qualifications can become a story about the economic impact of under-prepared school leavers coming onto the job market.

As the business section of the newspaper has become more important, the layout and design of the newspaper have changed. Editors of the business section need to explain difficult concepts in a visually appealing way and have brought more colour, charts and diagrams into newspapers to clarify stories.

The state of the economy, locally or nationally, affects people either directly or indirectly. Increased or decreased budgets and different economic trends can affect employment and development. Readers wish to know what is going on as the state of the economy affects everyone.

Business stories may expose frauds or show how pressure groups are lobbying big business. It is very difficult to write on business without dealing with politics. Politics and business are absolutely intertwined.

Types of business stories

There are many different kinds of business stories. You will report on meetings, speeches, interviews, lawsuits, labour disputes, shareholders' meetings, stock prices, new industries, new taxes and duties, new products and developments. The list is endless. A lot of business reporting involves you in *interpretation*, in other words, you will be explaining *how* and *why* to your readers.

How to cover business news

The most important form of business reporting is interpreting for readers how a certain new event or decision will affect them directly. If a new industry is to be established or an industry is to be closed down in an area, what will be the effect on employment, housing, development and services in that area and surrounding areas? What would be the impact of a new pipeline, for example? Will it affect the environment? Will people be displaced to build it? What will be the direct impact on the local community? Sometimes it is difficult to find the local angle, but in almost every case that angle is there.

It is important to *explain or clarify business jargon* for your readers so that they can understand. The *Wall Street Journal*, one of the most successful newspapers in the world, has made a success of taking complex business and economic issues and making them accessible to all its readers no matter what their standard of education. The *Wall Street Journal's* style of writing and reporting has been copied by newspapers around the world (see Chapter 10).

The following quote summarises the main work of business reporting:

> "The most important form of interpretation in reporting the economic life of a community is that which reaches below the surface of events and brings forth significances and trends. The stockmarket figures, commodity prices, car loadings and other financial data are usually not significant in themselves. Compared with what they were a year ago or last month, they may have a meaning and be a prophecy of the future." [43.]

You can probably see that a journalist should be cautious about making economic predictions because the results of this could be serious. People may react to a journalist's advice or prediction with disastrous results.

When covering strikes and lockouts, a journalist must remain neutral and interpret the events in an objective way. Because labour issues are often explosive, labour stories must be carefully balanced. It is important to remember that the basis of any strike or lockout is a disagreement between labour and management and the story should always focus on that disagreement and its resolution.

General reporting

The *general assignment reporter* obviously does not have a specific beat. This reporter does not know what assignment the working day will bring. The news editor can tell them (at a moment's notice) to cover any event that has just occurred. General assignment reporters therefore have to be versatile and able to think on their feet. They often need to travel long distances to cover stories so they should always be prepared for any outcome.

Conclusion

In this chapter, you learnt the role of both the general assignment and the beat reporter. You learnt the requirements and demands of the various beats and what special skills you require to cover a specific beat.

Suggested Reading

1.   Berry, Thomas Elliot, *Journalism in America*, New York, Hasting House Publishers, 1976.

2.   Brooks, Brian S, *et al*, *The Missouri Group, News Reporting & Writing*, New York, St Martins Press, 4th edition, 1992.

3.   Harris, Geoffrey, *Journalism Media Manual – Practical Newspaper Reporting*, 2nd ed, Focal Press, 1993.

4.   Nel, Francois, *Writing for the Media,* Southern Book Publishers, 1994.

5.   Teel, Leonard R, *et al, Into the Newsroom – An introduction to journalism*, Prentice-Hall, 1983.

6.   Ward, Hiley H, *Professional Newswriting*, New York, Harcourt Brace Jovanovich Publishers, 1985.

Investigative journalism –
13   digging in dark places

 Introduction

There have been many famous examples of investigative journalism. The most famous one is probably the investigative work done by *Washington Post* reporters, Carl Bernstein and Bob Woodward, when they exposed the corruption of the Nixon administration in the *Watergate* affair. In South Africa we have a number of excellent examples of great investigative journalism: for example, Mervyn Rees and Chris Day's investigation of the 'information scandal' and Jacques Pauw's work on the 'death squads'.

Most journalism students probably want to become investigative or political journalists. They feel that there is excitement and romance in this kind of journalism. People see investigative journalists as the 'cowboys' of the journalism world. They seem to be the 'do-gooders' or heroes, who fight evil and put things right. Investigative journalism also seems to be the one area where a journalist can win awards and the admiration of the public.

Sadly, the real life of the investigative journalist is very different. Their work can be the most difficult and the loneliest form of journalism there is. Days, weeks and even years of tracking down leads and building up a story may prove fruitless. Investigative journalists may have to fight for editorial support. Also people often threaten them and try to pressure them not to continue or publish. The truth is not welcome to many powerful people.

 Outcome

By the end of this chapter, you will understand why there is a need for investigative journalism. You will also know about the obstacles that investigative journalists face, and the difficulties in obtaining information. Finally, you will understand the importance of doing follow-ups.

5 Minute Task

> *Before you read on:*
> - *Find a copy of a newspaper like the **Mail and Guardian** or **The Sunday Independent**.*
> - *Find an investigative story, e.g. a story that has dug up the truth about corruption, injustice, etc.*
> - *Read it carefully. Look for signs of any or all of the following:*
>   - *who the reporter had to find and interview and how this person/people responded*
>   - *what documents the reporter had to find*
>   - *what places the reporter had to go to, and how*
>   - *what threats or dangers the reporter had to face*
>   - *how long he/she had to work on the story*
>   - *what costs the newspaper must have had to pay for*
> - *Now think about what obstacles and pressures that reporter must have faced, and list the*
>   - *qualities the reporter needed to have as a person.*
>   - *motives the reporter had in doing that story.*

What is investigative journalism?

Investigative journalism is the quest for the truth. It is the job of bringing hidden facts to light and then finding out how they connect. The investigative journalist must spend more time on digging for facts and less time on looking for an interesting story angle than another journalist would. Investigative journalism gives the journalist social responsibility to light up dark places. The public expects these journalists to examine people like government officials and important public issues critically [very searchingly, evaluating them carefully]. One kind of task for these journalists is to show where the achievements of government programmes do not match the claims and promises of government officials. For example, in South Africa, the claims of government officials on housing generally do not correspond with their delivery of housing.

Where do investigative journalists get information? Information normally comes from sources within the organisation where the wrong or misdeed under investigation is being committed. In Chapter 4 we discussed such sources. There are a number of *leakers* [sources] of information such as the *Animus Leaker* – that is, the source (usually a politician) who uses a leak to spite or embarrass another person or party. Perhaps you will also remember the *Whistle-blower* described in Chapter 4. This is someone like a civil servant who 'leaks' when they feel that they can't put something right in the usual way. In this case, the leakers are often willing to make a public statement and be named, although they may risk losing their jobs.

The need for investigative journalism

Without investigative journalists, the world would be a far more corrupt place where truth and democracy would battle to exist.

The influential German sociologist, Ferdinand Tonnies, wrote:

> *"The press is the real instrument of public opinion, a weapon and a tool in the hands of those who know how to use it; it possesses universal power as the dreaded critic of events and changes in social conditions. It is comparable and, in some respects, superior to the material power which the states possess through their armies, their treasuries and their bureaucratic civil service."* **44.**

And according to Ray Mungo:

> *"Facts are less important than truth and the two are far from equivalent... for cold facts are nearly always boring and may even distort the truth, but Truth is the highest achievement of human expression."* **45.**

One could say that the investigative journalist has a social responsibility to dig up evidence of corruption and wrongdoing. He/she must publish such evidence so that the perpetrators can be brought to justice either in a court of law or in the court of public opinion. The investigative journalist must report the facts with complete accuracy and must therefore dig behind the facts to understand their context. The former *Rand Daily Mail*, which closed in 1985, used this approach in an exemplary way. It had an admirable record as a champion of human rights and a voice for black interests and perspectives. This made it very unpopular with the Nationalist government of the day.

The *Mail's* finest contribution to journalism in South Africa was its coverage of the 1976 Soweto riots and the 'Information scandal'. The *Rand Daily Mail* at the time played a unique bridging role between blacks and whites as a forum where ideas could be shared. It pioneered [started] a particular style in South African journalism in that it initiated many searching exposés of government abuses and stood firmly and unambiguously against what it saw as the dishonesties and injustices of the apartheid society.

Lighting up dark places.

Because of this courageous approach the *Mail* gained the respect of the black population and the late Percy Qoboza, doyen [senior member] of South Africa's black editors said:

> "*The* **Mail** *was not just another paper; it was an institution, a courageous crusader for justice and peace. Far ahead of white public opinion, it gave us the courage to go on."* **46.**

Constraints on investigative journalism

Not all newspapers do investigative reporting and in South Africa investigative reporting is the exception rather than the rule. The *Mail & Guardian* and to some extent *The Sunday Times* stand out as two publications that are prepared to do what it takes to unearth wrong doing and corruption. The *Independent Group* also have a small investigative unit.

You will find that even bold investigative journalists face many obstacles before their investigative story reaches the public. Even their own courage and convictions can weaken.

The first constraint is the *cost of investigative journalism,* which is the most costly form of journalism. It takes time and money and few newspapers can afford the expense. Can you imagine the cost to a newspaper (in salaries and other costs) of an investigation which takes more than a few days?

The second constraint is *manpower.* Most newspapers are under-staffed and cannot afford to have one of their best journalists tied up on one story for a long time.

The third constraint is *a failure of courage or the lack of will from the editor to publish the story.* Editors may fear the legal and social repercussions [results and responses] that they will face once the story breaks. Investigative reporting upsets people and normally the people who get the most upset are important and powerful. It takes courage to stand up to such people and cope with the pressure they may apply. Quite often investigative reporters receive threats on their lives and even their families' lives. The government might use other forms of intimidation, for example, during the Watergate affair the Nixon administration threatened the *Washington Post's* lucrative [profitable] television licenses.

The fourth constraint *is the threat by advertisers to withdraw advertising.* This usually only works where the newspaper is under severe financial difficulties and has strong competition.

The fifth constraint is simply *trying to convince your editor that the story deserves to be covered.* To do effective investigative journalism you need resources, time and money. Your editor must therefore be willing to support you and publish the story.

Doing the investigation

What starts a journalist off on a piece of investigative journalism? Well, most investigations begin after *a tip-off from a source* (see Chapters 4 and 5 for more details on this), or because the journalist gets a *hunch* [a strong suspicion or guess]. There has to be some basis for beginning an investigation.

After receiving a tip-off or when following-up on a hunch, it is best to do some preliminary investigations before forming a *hypothesis*.

The *hypothesis* (see Chapter 6) is a statement that you believe to be true and will then prove or disprove by your investigations. For example, your hypothesis could be, *New houses are being allocated to the friends of government officials*. Making a hypothesis allows you to focus on the main point of what you want to investigate and removes any confusion about what is being investigated.

Although you intend to prove your hypothesis, you must be open to the possibility that you may not be able to do so. *Maintain an open mind* and do not ignore evidence that may disprove your hypothesis. Doing so is the mark of a bad journalist.

The first part of the investigation, which should only take a day or two, is to determine whether or not you have a chance to prove your hypothesis. Are you able to obtain the information you need to prove your hypothesis?

Once you have decided that you can prove your hypothesis you have to ask the question: *Is there a story here?* If your answer *is yes* you need to ask the question: *Can I get this story?*

Finally, you should ask the question: *Who gives a damn?* If you decide that no-one cares about the issue, you are probably wasting your time investigating it.

Difficulties in obtaining information

Poor planning can lead to difficulties in your investigation. Good investigative journalism requires good planning and organisation. Sometimes you obtain so much information that you are unable to 'see the wood for the trees'. It is important to keep asking: *Does the information obtained help prove or disprove your hypothesis?* Draw up an action plan and carry it out; do not get sidetracked on issues that are not relevant to the hypothesis. Remember, investigative journalism costs money and your editor will want to see some progress if you are asking for sufficient time to complete your investigation.

Difficulties can arise if you risk the confidentiality of your sources. If this happens, and even if the source only suspects that it will happen, you may lose a valuable source as well as some of your own credibility. Remember to keep your source's names confidential so that you protect your sources even if your notes or files are subpoenaed.

Ethical difficulties can arise when you dig for information. Remember the *Code of Conduct,* which states: *'A journalist shall obtain information, photographs and illustrations only by straightforward means. The use of other means can be justified only by the overriding considerations of the public interest. The journalist is entitled to exercise a personal conscientious objection to the use of such means.'*

One of the biggest difficulties in obtaining information is in *dealing with witnesses who are reluctant to talk.* This reluctance often comes from their fear of losing their jobs. How can we get reluctant people to talk, bearing in mind that they have a right *not* to talk? You can use positive reinforcement statements such as: *It would be in the best interests of others...* or, *Wouldn't you prefer it if something like this didn't happen to others...?* Sometimes this approach will encourage interviewee participation.

Checking facts

Accuracy is important in all reporting and it is absolutely essential to investigative reporting. Inaccurate reporting can lead to legal action and embarrassment which can detract from the good work the investigation has achieved. Those who have implicated in wrong-doing only require one small loophole to destroy the good work done.

Remember the golden rule: *Check your facts, then check them again*; because there is no excuse for error. During the Watergate investigations the *Washington Post* used a strict policy on accuracy. They checked two independent sources before they published any allegation.

Facts may indeed be *a mixture of what can be discovered and what can be deduced* [worked out from the evidence available]. But this must not become *'what can be invented'*.

Following up

It is not always possible to know what reaction an investigative report will receive. People want to trust government and public figures, after all, that is why they voted them into power.

Even when there is overwhelming evidence against a public figure(s), the public may want to give perpetrator(s) the benefit of the doubt. For the investigative journalist, this can be a bitter pill to swallow. You may not be prepared for the overall public reaction to your expose and if the response is negative you may not feel motivated to continue with your investigation. However, an important part of being a journalist who brings unwelcome news to the public is being able to *handle the flak*.

On the other side of the coin, once a story has broken you are likely to receive new leads, particularly from people who were too scared to talk before. It is now important to keep up the pressure, and also to sustain your motivation and your editor's motivation too.

Editors often lose interest once the initial excitement of a story has died down, although there may be important follow-up that could be done.

5 Minute Task

> Look back to the investigative story you chose for the first task in this chapter. Consider:
> • Was this story closed by the end or did it need more follow-up? What aspects needed follow up?
> (If necessary, apply the above test to several other investigative stories too.)
> • What obstacles may the reporter face in following up this particular story/stories, in your opinion?

Conclusion

Investigative journalism can be considered the heart of journalism and is basically a quest for the truth. It is the job of bringing hidden facts to light and setting them in relation to one another. Investigative journalism requires the journalist to be critical and to dig persistently for facts, even when faced with difficulties, threats and resistance, and even when the public may not be ready to accept what perpetrators of wrong have done.

Suggested Reading

1. Altschull, Herbert J, *Agents of Power*, Longman, New York, 1984.

2. Brooks, Brian S, *et al*, *The Missouri Group, News Reporting & Writing*, New York, St Martins Press, 4th edition, 1992.

3. Jackson, Gordon S, *Breaking Story – The South African Press*, Westview Press, Boulder, 1993.

4. Nel, Francois, *Writing for the Media*, Southern Book Publishers, 1994.

Development

14   journalism

Introduction

This chapter is basically about the amount of freedom the media should have, that is, should they be able to publish whatever they wish to publish, at any time, or should there be controls and limits on this? In particular, how should they treat the government of the country? And, looking even more closely, how should they treat the government of a developing country? In such a case, the government may have a difficult development task to do, because there is poverty and a shortage of different resources. The support of the media may be important to them in performing this task.

Several theories have strongly influenced the way the press in Africa has responded to questions like the above. In this chapter, we will look at the three theories that have dominated the press in Africa, that is, the theories of *authoritarianism, social responsibility* and *development*. We will also look briefly at the libertarian theory and see how this has impacted on [affected] the other three. Finally we will look at the advantages and problems of developmental journalism for the media.

Outcome

At the end of this chapter, you should be able to demonstrate the differences between the theory of authoritarianism and the theory of responsibility. You should also be able to explain how these two approaches relate to the developmental approach to journalism. Furthermore, you should understand both the advantages and disadvantages of the developmental approach to journalism.

5 Minute Task

> *Before you read on, consider the following points (discuss them, with a partner or group if possible):*
> * *Do you think that the media should be able to publish anything at all, or should there be controls over what can be published? Why?/Why not?*

- *If you think there should be control over what can be published, what kind of controls do you think there should be? Who should exercise control?*
- *Do you think that the media should be basically supportive of the government of a country or not? Why?/Why not? Now read on.*

Authority or social responsibility?

The authoritarian theory

The authoritarian theory of the press has always been popular with colonial governments in Africa. This was also true in South Africa, and many people might say that the old Nationalist government did its best to put the authoritarian theory into practice.

Why? What makes the authoritarian view so popular? This theory says that *the media are in the service of the state and therefore subordinate to* [under] *the state*. They should do nothing which could undermine [harm] established authority. Rather, the media must support the interests of the state at all costs.

Because the authoritarian view holds that the state is more important than the individual, it also says that the individual can only achieve his/her goals if he/she is under the state. However, different individuals within an authoritarian state have different status [importance]. Some individuals do have much importance. For example, the leader of an authoritarian state may be one person or an elite [high-class, leading] group who dominate the society. This kind of leadership uses the the mass media to help them dominate the rest of the society, that is, the media are used as *instruments of social control*.

In an authoritarian society, truth is limited and not all individuals have access to it. Most people have to accept the 'truth' of the dominant person or group and must conform to [fit in with] this 'truth' in their thoughts and actions.

To stay in power, the leadership of the authoritarian state will use any means of persuading or forcing others that they consider necessary. At different times we have seen examples of this in Africa – in South Africa, Zimbabwe and Kenya. In this kind of society, the ruling elite use the press as an educational and propaganda tool for controlling the people. They tolerate no criticism of the government. They do not see objectivity and truth as the most important principles guiding the media. Their view is that the interests of the state must come first, and they, the ruling elite, must decide what these interests are.

Libertarian theory

The social responsibility theory was born in the middle of the twentieth century and developed from the libertarian theory when some people started to feel that the press could no longer be allowed to function entirely freely. So, what was the libertarian theory?

The libertarian theory said that the media was no longer just an instrument of the state. Libertarians believed that we are rational beings, able to distinguish right from wrong. Furthermore, they believed that society should create a forum, *a free market of ideas* so that people could look at different ideas and then choose freely. Therefore, *the libertarians believed that there should be no formal controls at all over what can be published in the press or other media.* Rather, they felt that where all ideas have an equal chance, truth will stand and win. The spreading of these ideas led to the acceptance of basic human rights such as freedom of speech and of the press.

According to libertarianism anyone with enough money could publish a newspaper. But then people began to see that the media could use information not to inform the public but rather just to increase the circulation of the newspapers. A new point of view developed which proposed that the press could no longer be allowed to function with total freedom.

Social responsibility theory

A new approach to the role of the media in society developed, namely, the social responsibility theory. In this theory, *objectivity is vitally important.* Supporters of this theory felt that it was closely linked to the libertarian theory. However, the social responsibility theory develops, changes and deepens certain ideas in libertarianism. After the Second World War, social responsibility 'swept the world as a standard to seek.'

Most English-language papers in South Africa have taken social responsibility as their guiding theory. During the apartheid era, various editors started to reject the strongly authoritarian control which the Nationalist party exerted over the press. These editors began to feel that the social responsibility theory could be a better guide for them. Their group included editors of English papers, and later, editors of alternative papers and also some Afrikaans editors. They were all looking to the social responsibility theory as the best for South African society. So, what is this theory?

Basically, *social responsibility theory emphasises the responsibility that the media has toward the society, more than it emphasises freedom.* It says that the media should work within certain moral and ethical limitations that are like obligations [duties, responsibilities] they must accept. *"These obligations are mainly to be met by setting high or professional standards of informativeness, truth, accuracy, objectivity and balance."* [47.]

According to this theory the media must accept social responsibility and make sure that different attitudes and directions of thought all get fully and properly represented and heard. The media must see to it that the public has enough information to make necessary decisions.

At the same time, *freedom is important in this theory.* It says that the media must guard against possible interference by the state and by any other pressure groups which could threaten the media's freedom. Control of the media should not be the job of an elite group in government. Rather, *the journalists themselves must exercise this social responsibility,* working for newspapers that are mostly privately owned. What guides the journalist who must exercise social responsibility? Journalists working with this theory generally try to reflect public opinion fully, but they may also sometimes try to form or guide public opinion.

This theory rejects the way authoritarianism makes control actually lawful so that the media has no freedom of choice. On the other hand, it also rejects a situation where there are no principles to limit and guide what the media can publish, that is, where they publish whatever they like and whatever will make the most money.

However the social responsibility theory has been criticised quite a lot. For example, according to Altschull:

> "the painful reality is that the term social responsibility is a term devoid of [without] meaning. Put another way, it is a term whose content is so vague that almost any meaning can be placed upon it. As such it, too, serves the ultimate end of social control ... Perhaps this is the reason one cannot find the term 'social responsibility' in the Oxford English Dictionary." [48.]

Although Altschull sees these problems and faults in the idea of social responsibility, he still suggests that it has value for the working journalist. First, it gives journalists a positive feeling that they are working in the public interest and doing a public service. Second, it frees journalists from writing only material that will sell well. They need not be slaves to whatever others say is in the interest of their readers.

What is development journalism?

The development theory became popular in the Third World for obvious reasons. However, there are some problems with the idea. Firstly, the terms *Third World, undeveloped nations* or *developing nations* seem to imply inferiority and something less than best. They seem to rate the *Third World's* industry, commerce and political life poorly against the industry, commerce and politics of the world's *great* nations.

Altschull believes that there are now so many different forms of the theory that there can be no single definition on which most people will agree. Because of this, and because *'development'* seems to imply inferiority, Altschull prefers the term *'advancing journalism.'*

What does the development theory postulate [state, propose]? Those who take this approach see the press as an instrument of social justice and a tool for achieving beneficial [positive, helpful] social change. In other words, 'the media should accept and carry out

positive development tasks in line with nationally established policy.'
There is an 'assumption that the press is seen as a two-way communication, with equal importance assigned to the writer and the reader, to the broadcaster and the listener.'

Sadly, in reality, things have not worked out in line with the theory.
In Africa generally there has been pressure on journalists to ally
themselves with the political forces. But in doing so they have lost
their independence.

*The most problematical part of the theory is the principle that the
state can interfere with the media* and use methods like censorship,
state subsidies or direct control and restriction if it does so in order to
advance development. In this way journalists can be severely ham-
pered from reporting fully, fairly and independently. Also, we cannot
be certain that development *does* get advanced in such situations.

Obviously, a new government in a developing country may well
wish to adopt the development model. It leaves control of the
media in the hands of the government if required and yet the
media must still take responsibility. If the government decides that
the media are not meeting its wishes or that they are challenging
the state, it can intervene and apply whatever censure or control it
deems necessary.

Zimbabwe is a good example of a government 'seeking to use the
press with some degree of compulsion to advance government
policies, especially on economic and racial or ethnic issues.'

Editors who accept this approach must give up some editorial autonomy [independent control] to government officials, and in doing so, they give up the constitutional right of freedom of the press. Journalists in South Africa have had a very unhappy experience with government authoritarianism in the past. Therefore, they will not easily trust any government uncritically or risk their autonomy in the way that the development approach requires. Their fears about doing so are based on what they have seen elsewhere. Thus, while the development system may offer benefits, journalists feel that it extracts too high a price.

Finally, *development journalism promotes mass rights over those of the individual*. It is rooted in the notion [idea] of doing what is right for the 'common good'. South Africans have fought hard for their new constitution that protects the rights of the individual and therefore it will be hard to promote the virtues of developmental journalism. However, that does not of course prevent the government of the day doing its best to get the press to report in a developmental way.

Advantages of development journalism

Development journalism has a lot of attraction for developing countries. First, in countries where poverty is the norm, the government of the day wants and needs as much support as it can get. A press which reports government inefficiencies is therefore not welcome. Also, the government will probably have to take decisions which are based on the common good but which harm individual liberties. These decisions may be highly unpopular but they have to be taken, and a hostile press can hold back government's progress. A supportive press can help the government to push these policies ahead.

How can a journalist best use this approach? According to Narinder Aggarwala, an executive in the United Nations Development Program, the duty of a journalist reporting on development is to:

*"critically examine, evaluate and report the relevance of
a development project to national and local needs, the
difference between a planned scheme and its actual
implementation, and the difference between its impact
on people as claimed by government officials, and as it
actually is."* [49.]

The most important function of development journalism is its ability
to *'nation build'*. Respected Kenyan political leader Tom Mboya
once told a gathering of journalists that the African press had to
serve the cause of nation building. Moreover, since the press served
an informative, critical and educational function, it had to be permit-
ted to operate in freedom and to join with African leaders in their
nation building efforts. On the other hand, Mboya charged that if
editors and journalists did not act accordingly they should be
charged as traitors, and many were.

Pitfalls of development journalism

The pitfalls of the development approach are many. First, the press
becomes less critical and eventually is forced to give up its 'watchdog'
role in society. As it continually panders to [serves, pleases] the
government, the media loses its critical edge and becomes nothing
more than another government mouthpiece. When this happens it
opens the way for a virulent [hostile, fierce and aggressive] under-
ground or alternative press with a strong anti-government approach.

The most dangerous pitfall is the fact that the press gives up its right
to question and demand accountability from the government of the
day. As the press tries to promote the government and the common
good, it can start to lose sight of the individual and the individual's
human rights. In other words:

*"A developmental press has come to be equated with
one in which the government exercises tight control and
prevents freedom of expression, all in the name of noble
ends."* [50.]

Government censorship does not happen in Africa and South America only. In 1975, Indira Gandhi imposed strict censorship in India. But despite this censorship,

> *"many Indian journalists sneaked into their news columns words, phrases and even sentences and paragraphs that escaped the attention of the censors and that conveyed concealed meanings to knowledgeable readers"*. [51.]

There are many other examples of editors and journalists resisting censorship. Overall, the message for any government is that it will have to struggle to keep up control of the media for very long, it will need huge resources to police this system. What starts out as a good idea to promote development seems to turn into a nightmare.

 # Conclusion

You have now considered the three theories that have dominated the press in Africa, that is, authoritarianism, social responsibility and development. You have learnt how libertarian theory impacted on the social responsibility theory. Finally you have looked at the advantages and pitfalls of development journalism for the media.

Suggested Reading

1.   Altschull, Herbert J, *Agents of Power*, Longman, New York, 1984.

2.   Jackson, Gordon S, *Breaking Story – The South African Press*, Westview Press, Boulder, 1993.

Different types of
15 newspapers

Introduction

As you know by now, there are several different kinds of news-papers. One kind of newspaper may be different from another in special ways. The differences may be due to which time of day the newspapers appear; how frequently they appear; their size and visual format; which readers they are targeting; how far the news-papers are read and distributed, and so on.

Outcome

By the time you have read this chapter, you should know about several different types of newspapers. You should understand what each kind is like and be able to recognise them. You should have an idea of the particular strengths of each type of newspaper, as well as some of its disadvantages.

10 Minute Task

Think about all the newspapers you know. What makes one newspaper different from another? Try to fit the newspapers you know into different types. Use the following criteria to help you classify each one:
- *when, and how often, it appears*
- *what different kinds of stories it carries*
- *where, and how far it gets distributed*
- *its (page) size, its thickness and its general appearance*
- *whether its readers pay for it or get it free*
- *what sort of reader it seems to be aimed at.*

Dailies

These, as the name suggests, are published on a daily basis. There are two kinds of daily, the morning edition, e.g. *The Sowetan, The Mercury,* and the late edition, e.g. *The Star* and *The Daily News.* The morning edition covers events from the day before publication while the late edition covers what happened during the day.

Weekly newspapers

These generally serve much smaller areas than daily newspapers and publish news that is more specific to an area, such as news of local business and politics. Most of these publications do not carry state, national or world news. *The Leader,* which is a *sectionalised* weekly [a weekly aimed at a particular section of the population], targets the Indian reader. *The Leader* does publish some news of foreign countries and governments such as India and Pakistan because this could interest its readers. But it may also report on local school events, high achievers in the community, or other items that a large daily paper would usually ignore.

In contrast, the *Mail & Guardian,* an international weekly tabloid, concentrates on the chief national and international events of the preceding week. Reporters on this kind of paper write mainly about 'news behind the news'. In other words, these reporters investigate and analyse events more deeply, linking facts to form a broader picture of an issue or issues. The *M & G* is distributed on a Friday and provides features, portraits, interviews, commentary, reportage, arts and theatre.

Weekend newspapers

Weekend newspapers such as *The Sunday Tribune, The Sunday Times, City Press,* and *Rapport* do report on the main national, international and regional news of the week. However, these publications also include leisure reading inserts such as *The Sunday Life* magazine and *The Other Mag.* In addition, papers like *The Sunday Times* and *The Sunday Tribune* have inserts which only appear in certain regions and are somewhat sectionalised, e.g. *The Metro* (in the *Tribune*), *Sunday Times Extra* and the *Gauteng Metro* in the *City Press.*

Weekend newspapers also cover many human interest stories to make the newspaper more appealing to the buyer. This kind of newspaper carries mostly soft news or 'froth' and offers ideas on how readers can spend their weekend leisure time.

News magazines

These concentrate on chief international and national events of the preceding week or two. Most news magazines are published on a fortnightly basis, e.g. *Time* magazine. These magazines carry editorials, opinion columns, features and entertainment articles.

All weekend and weekly newspapers attract a wide variety of advertisers, and sell widely, too. They have created a profitable, secure *niche* [a safe market] for themselves although many people thought that the electronic media would put them out of business.

Tabloids and broadsheets

There are two major *sizes* of newspaper:
1. *Standard/broadsheet* – pages measure about 38 by 58 cm
2. *Tabloid* – about half the size.

These two types of paper are different in other ways as well as in size and appearance. Some people would even say that tabloid newspapers are not true newspapers, because both their content and their physical form are a change from the more traditional broadsheet style. Both tabloids and broadsheets are still based on text, but tabloids are more strongly visual.

Tabloids run items across two pages more often than broadsheets do. This can make the page-as-unit [the overall page] similar to a broadsheet page, but the amount of information included differs.

A tabloid cannot have as many illustrations as a broadsheet because these would compete with one another for the reader's attention. This would produce a crowded, confused effect on the smaller tabloid page.

A typical tabloid front page is a window to the inside of the tabloid. It could use large colour photographs sometimes taking up almost all of the front page as in the *Daily Mirror* or a large colour illustration on almost a third of the page as in the *Daily Mail.*

Many broadsheet publications have tabloid sections, for example, television listings, entertainment guides, special news reports. There is more discussion about the tabloid design in Chapter 16.

Within a broadsheet newspaper, the most important visual element is positioned above the *fold* [on the top half of the page] or across the fold. The reader's eye should be able to wander at random [freely, without a set direction] over the broadsheet page. Because this page has many items fitted together, readers can cover a number of news items side by side on the page.

Community newspapers

Target: Community newspapers are newspapers that target certain communities within a specific region. The community could be a *geographical* community, that is, the community within a specific area in which the newspaper is distributed. On the other hand, the community could be a community of *interest*, that is, community members who have a common understanding. Obviously, the news in such papers should appeal to those communities.

Some community newspapers are formed by companies who see an opportunity to target communities that they feel are not well-served by their newspapers. These newspapers cater for their specific areas. For example, in KwaZulu-Natal, the *North Coast Courier* caters for the north coast areas like La Mercy, Stanger, Mandeni, etc. and the *Highway Mail* caters for the areas around Pinetown, such as, Hillcrest, Kloof, New Germany and Westville. The *Northern Natal Courier* covers for Dundee, Glencoe, Vryheid, etc.

Popular, or just free?: Community newspapers rely heavily on advertising and some of them are distributed free. Even for those that are sold, sales cannot make enough money to generate income and sustain the newspaper. Free community newspapers obviously appeal to those people who cannot afford to buy newspapers. Moreover, advertisers are keen to get their messages across to these people.

Types of story: There is often a large gap between local newspapers as they are in reality and the ideal community newspaper that one imagines. In its news package, a successful community newspaper will generally emphasise human interest, and stories should always have local relevance. That is, a community newspaper should always get a local angle for any story that relates to national news. If there is no direct impact locally, the national story won't have much importance for readers.

Many community newspapers do publish developmental stories about Reconstruction and Development Programme (RDP) projects, local councils projects and other community related matters such as crime in the community, community role-models, achievers, etc.

The reality vs the ideal: These newspapers also often claim to have 100 per cent readership. However, this does not mean that they really respond to community interests and needs and have loyal readers as a result. The truth is that they are usually delivered from door-to-door, to ensure that they reach the readers and thus serve the advertisers which keep them going. Seventy per cent or even more of such a newspaper may be taken up by advertising.

In addition, many South African 'community' newspapers do not cater for all their supposed readers. They write for their advertisers, their suburban readers or local more affluent farmers, but do not cater for township readers. Quite frequently a local community newspaper will run a lead story about the achievements of a particular local industry that is a public relations exercise. Yet a real local news story that has national importance may be placed on the second or third page of the paper. Perhaps this story won't appear at all.

Some local publications lack even human interest stories, excepting possibly stories announcing forth-coming events and sports results. There may not even be much council news in the publication. Many such papers avoid controversy or investigative reporting, although there may be important and explosive developmental, environmental or other issues locally. Feature articles and reviews are scarce, and many papers do not have any freelance writers.

When I asked some of my own students to analyse some local Kwa-Zulu-Natal newspapers, they came up with many disturbing observations like those above. It became clear that some local papers do not see themselves as real newspapers at all. This appears in their lack of news-consciousness described above, and it also shows up in other small ways, for example, some papers do not even offer the names and contact details of the editor or staff in their pages. Stories do not have bylines, and readers are not encouraged to write or telephone with news or opinions.

However, some community newspapers do carry development stories, community announcements, local community sports news, and some hard-hitting local investigative stories as well as human interest stories. Some newspapers do use people from the community as reporters.

Size and format: Most community newspapers are tabloid size. Studies show little consistency in length, it changes, depending on the amount of advertising and/or news available. Stories are usually short, in some cases, a lead story may be less than 250 words. Also, as indicated above, there are rather few stories in most 'community' newspapers. An eight-page newspaper may have as little as 25 stories. Advertisements generally dominate the pages, except for the first page. Photographs are often placed for advertising rather than news purposes.

The alternative press

The alternative press is a way of describing those newspapers that take a different or opposite approach to the approaches that dominate the major newspapers and other media. The difference in approach is usually political. However, most alternative newspapers reflect not only different political opinions but also different parts of society and different life styles. Sometimes when there is a change of government, a newspaper that has been quite strongly 'alternative' under the previous government may become more 'mainstream'. However many alternative newspapers emphasise their special, independent style and their critical approach under all circumstances.

Those involved in the alternative press in some way will generally describe it as a lively and influential form of press. It took its place in South African society in the 1980s when apartheid and white supremacy were still in place.

The South African government of that time made strong verbal attacks on the alternative press, in and out of Parliament. They used legal and administrative measures to threaten, silence and intimidate the staff of such publications. Politicians tried everything to close them, but fortunately did not succeed. The alternative press used their skills to mirror the major changes in South Africa during the 80s.

Although alternative publications were small with a limited circulation they were very influential. Some people saw them as examples of what the future press of South Africa might be like.

The two most popular alternative papers in Johannesburg were the *Weekly Mail* and the *Vrye Weekblad*. Interestingly, both papers were directed mainly by whites. Most of their readers were liberal and affluent [well-off]. The *Mail* started in 1985 and came to be seen as the most professionally produced paper. The *Vrye Weekblad* was the only Afrikaans alternative newspaper and was produced mainly by Afrikaners. Both papers dealt with social and political issues and were nationally distributed.

Some of the other alternative newspapers were:
1.   *The Indicator* which was located in an Indian residential area, and dealt with political coverage of interest to that community.

2.   *The New Nation* which was more African-orientated and openly allied itself with the African National Congress and their ideals.

3.   *South* was based in Cape Town and was read mainly by Africans and coloureds.

4.   *The New African* which catered for the black and Indian population.

Because making a profit was not their main objective, the alternative media often experienced problems with advertising. They often relied on outside funding which did not always come through.

The school press

The idea of a school press is usually to stimulate young people in the development of communication skills. It should prepare them for careers within newspapers, magazines and other information publications and agencies. A school newspaper may reflect achievements and record school events. The contributors to the school newspaper should be mainly those students who are interested in the print medium. A teacher or teachers usually guides the editorial team of learners.

A school newspaper usually gets published once a month, due to lack of resources and the fact that most of its writers are busy with their studies. It usually contains not more than four pages and offers mainly information on school events, new developments within the school and interesting trivia. Most school newspapers don't contain hard hitting or investigative stories. There is no reason why this situation should not change, although of course problems can arise if learners tackle real school and community issues.

The learner readers of a school newspaper prefer a light, informal style. The learners who write for the paper are also writing for their peers. These learners can act as editors and decide as a collective what should feature in their publication for that specific month.

Most school newspapers use simple layout that is not much guided by design. Cartoons or drawings can add interest to the pages. The paper is usually copied or printed in black-and-white.

As a school newspaper circulates only within a school community, it could be difficult to attract advertisers. Adverts and sponsorships are however sometimes obtained for the school magazine, which is an annual publication.

The student press

The school press and student publications at universities and technikons are of course related in various ways. The student media at tertiary level cater for a larger target audience, generally focus on harder hitting issues and have far greater power to bring about change in an institution. The student press is usually much better resourced with sponsorship, facilities and a larger pool of talented writers to draw on.

Because contributors to a student paper come from different faculties and groupings within the institution, they can reflect this diversity in their paper. Also, publications at this level are read and appreciated by a larger community including the staff.

A student paper should not align itself with any political organisation on campus, since this can destroy its credibility. Papers like *Dome* (published by students at the University of Natal, Durban) have a high ranking reputation amongst journalists, after winning the *Mail & Guardian's* 'best student publication' award in 1997. This paper contains both hard hitting and soft news, as well as investigative pieces and features. Their main focus is telling the story, and therefore their writers behave like any journalist working for a commercial newspaper.

A university or technikon publication is distributed among students who have different interests. Not every student will be interested in hearing about the latest technological defect in computers, or the fact that disputes can only be resolved through communication. A student paper must appeal to students as well as to advertisers. The student press does attract a fair amount of advertisers but it sometimes battles to keep its advertising sponsorship going. For this reason, student publications have to insure that their expenditure is well within their allocated budget, and as they are acting as management of their own publication, they have to be financially and ethically responsible.

In-house publications

A *house journal* can be seen as a general-interest newspaper. It can also be defined as an organisational publication or a corporate publication. Most of these journals are published in an A4 format with advertisements which cover costs. It is basically a publication which does not aim to make a profit, through which an organisation communicates with its internal or external target audiences at least twice a year. The basic objective of a house journal is to communicate and provide valuable information and hence contribute to the productivity of the company.

It provides information for reference purposes, can be read in employees' spare time and may also involve the families in the organisation. The editorial policy of a house journal usually fits in with the mission or objectives of the organisation, that is the 'company culture'.

Specialist publications

A specialist publication usually focuses on a particular subject and therefore has a *niche market*. These publications are necessary for people who have particular interests and because they are so specialised they require much research and time to produce. Specialist publications include papers covering sport, technology, the arts, fashion, crime and many other areas. Sport is possibly the biggest area of specialisation.

5 Minute Task

> *Check through the task you did before reading this chapter.*
> *Now that you know more about different types of newspapers,*
> *make any alterations to your classification of newspapers that*
> *seem necessary.*
> * *Were any of the types of newspapers described in the*
>   *chapter new to you?*
> * *Which kind of newspaper would you prefer to work on and*
>   *why?*
> * *Which types of newspaper are the most useful to society, in*
>   *your opinion? Why do you say this?*

Conclusion

The media exist throughout our society and influence us at every level. Publications, no matter in what form or design, should enlighten, educate and inform the people they target. Some of the types of publication described in this chapter are not mainstream media. However, many of these do reach the readers they aim to reach, and do manage to inform and educate and therefore fulfil their purposes.

Design & layout –

16   getting it to look right

 ## Introduction

Since desk top publishing and computer-to-plate printing appeared, journalists often have to layout a story within an allocated space on a page. The modern journalist therefore needs a good understanding of the principles of design and layout.

 ## Outcome

After studying this chapter, you will understand what design and layout are. You will know the typography terms that you use when you design and layout a publication. You will also understand the role of pictures in a publication. Finally, you will know how to edit pictures.

What is design and layout?

Whether you are involved with a student publication or a major daily newspaper, you will find that design is very important. What do we mean by *design* in newspapers and magazines? It is *the art of planning what the whole publication will look like and what its general layout will be.* Design affects every aspect of a publication from text to advertising, headlines and photography. Some people don't realise that design even includes the way we write and approach stories.

5 Minute Task

> Imagine that you have been made editor of a new student publication. Before you read any more of this chapter, brainstorm some ideas on:
> - what you would name the publication
> - what kind of visual design you would choose for the front page and throughout
> - why you would use this kind of design.

As you read the instructions for the task, you probably got some ideas about the design of your publication immediately. But, no matter what exciting ideas you may have, you as editor have to produce a publication that *communicates with your readership.* Unread articles just waste a little ink and a lot of effort. The design must draw fellow-students to the publication and make them loyal readers. The publication must become part of their lives, something that they cannot do without.

Why purpose and readership come first: Good design communicates with its readers. Therefore, everyone involved in the design effort must consider the purpose and readership of the publication. They must focus as a team on the design that will suit the purpose and readership. There are no special formulas or theories on how to design the perfect publication. What works in one market may not work in another. Before starting to *redesign* a publication that is not working, it is important to study the readership *demographics* [statistical and other information about the different groups of readers] and question the publication's content. If you don't do this, your exciting new design may only be dressing up a dead horse.

How layout works in design: *Layout is the way the design of a publication is expressed in each specific story and the combination of stories on the page.* As the the staff layout the newspaper, they have to solve the space problem raised by each story. They must use the special style rules of their publication to make that story look clear, interesting and memorable. If the design is successful, readers will be unaware that design features are attracting them and guiding them through the publication. But they will buy this readable publication again.

How design shows meaning: However, it is important to understand that good design and layout do not only make a paper *look* good. *Design also indicates meaning.* For example, different sizes of headline and pictures show which stories are more or less important. How important a story is can also be indicated by its position on the page and the page's position in the publication.

How design gives a paper identity: Design must give a publication its own *visual identity,* something that people will recognise.

So, who are we designing for? We are designing for our readers. We are designing to attract and hold the reader's attention against competition. This competition comes not only from other publications but also from other forms of media. We should not forget that while a good design will attract readers, only good content will keep them. In short, you cannot use good design to cover up bad journalism.

The best publications are those that have excellent content, look good, have a loyal readership and sell well. Unfortunately, there is no magic formula for achieving this. Some people have a strange idea that a publication of substance [a 'high quality' publication] should not make money. This is nonsense. Publishing (like any other type of business) must make a profit and a journalist should always remember this. In order to produce quality content and design but also make a profit, many people involved in the publication (including the journalist and even the reader) may have to make compromises.

Design basics

Good design is thus part of what makes for a successful publication. How do we arrive at a publication that works for all concerned – readers, journalists and owners? Here are some of the basics for good design:

1. The type size used and the width of columns must make the publication easy to read.

2. The contents of each page must be arranged to show very clearly which items are the most important.

3. The presentation of the words and pictures must be memorable, that is, readers must be able to remember the important points with little effort.

4. The presentation must also be clear so the reader does not struggle to understand the journalist's message.

Broadly, good design can contribute powerfully towards producing a publication that works, a publication that has a clear identity, a solid reputation and an acceptable balance between editorial and advertising. Advertisers look for such publications because they know that by advertising in them they will reach their target markets.

Satisfying the reader

For a design to work it must attract and satisfy present readers and possible *future* readers. *Blurbs* [short descriptions] and *teaser boxes* can direct readers towards information that they may want. Remember that readers also want to reach this information fast, they don't want to search for it. Complicated stories must be written and illustrated in such a way that they become easy to follow. *Colour* can help to organise and highlight text, *headlines* should be bold and readable and layout should indicate clearly what belongs to what. Readers must be able to *scan* the publication [look quickly over it, searching for key information] and still obtain all the important points in the news. Below are some different ways to achieve success in these aspects.

Page planning

A publication that communicates with its readers will have a clearly defined design pattern which is based on columns of text. The white space that surrounds the columns of text on a page is called the *margins*. The white space between the columns is known as the *gutter* and this space is usually much narrower than the width of the margins. To keep uniformity [keep to the same style] in a publication, the size of the margins and the gutters must be standard.

There is no ideal number of columns for a publication but most tabloids have between four and seven columns and broadsheets have between eight and ten columns. A standardised format also makes it easier for advertisers to design adverts that can be used in different publications.

Obviously, narrower columns are easier and faster to read but the limit is reached when the words begin to break up badly to keep inside the column width. Quality newspapers which rely on good writing with less pictures and illustrations often use broader columns.

Popular papers, on the other hand, prefer narrower columns which require less reading time. So you can see that the design and the number of columns gets chosen to suit the readership and the content of the publication.

When designing a page layout, the designer *imposes* [sets] a particular style of presentation in a publication. The designer uses columns, text, headlines, pictures and adverts as part of this style. The designer will normally design a number of *dummy* [draft, rough example] layouts so the layout team can try out different ideas.

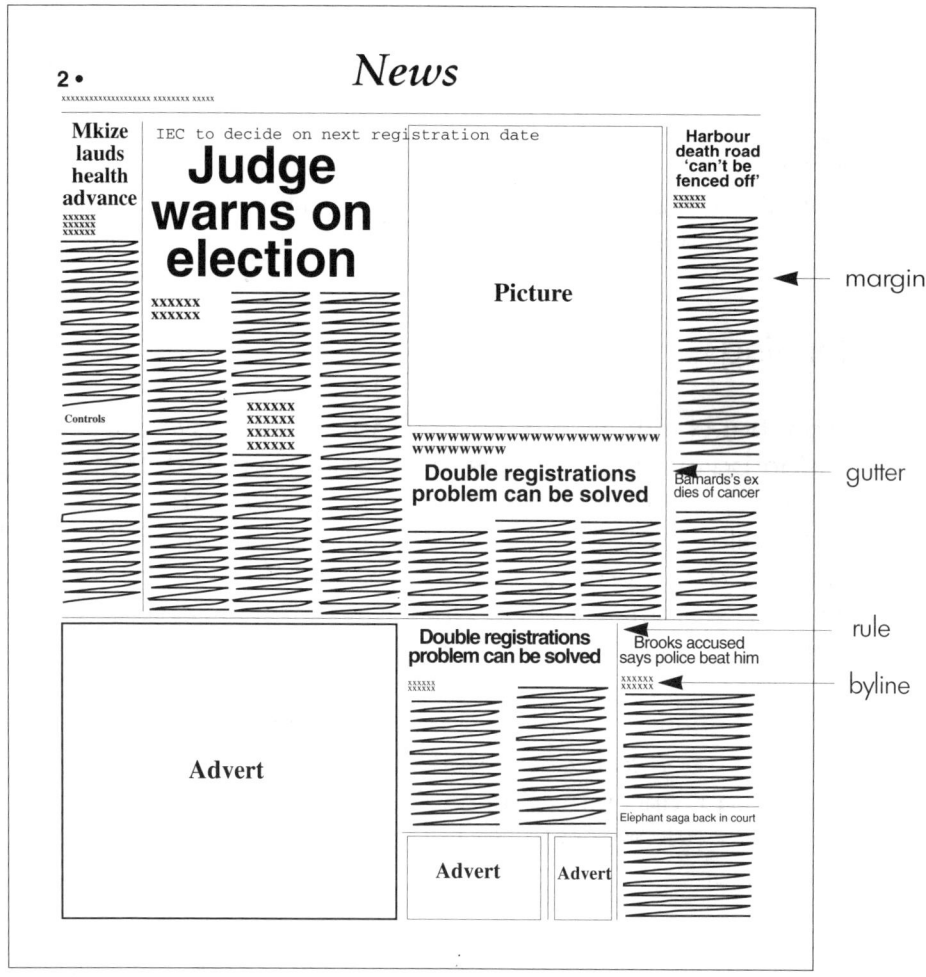

It is normal to subdivide a dummy page into a *grid*. This means that the page is subdivided vertically into columns and horizontally into modules so that each module [block] can hold a given number of lines of type. This shows clearly what space is available for pictures and text.

What must the page designer strive for?

Balance: Most newspapers today use a *modular* design. This means that each story (i.e. the copy, the headlines, the photos and the graphics used) must form a single four-cornered module that fits the page grid. Story modules must be balanced – small story equals small headline and small picture and vice versa. Do not place a small story module in the most prominent spot.

Consistency: Use no more than four typefaces – one for copy and three for headlines.

Contrast: There must be contrast on the page to create interest and tension. Do not however, create too much variety/contrast on the page. You do not want to draw your readers' eyes to and fro across the page, but rather from top left to bottom right.

Emphasis: Big headlines and pictures draw attention and say *Look at me*. They send a clear message to the reader about how you want them to read the page.

Clarity: Everything on the page must be clear and defined.

 5 Minute Task

> *Compare the two covers on page 202 and the example of a news page on page 200. Do you consider them good examples of what a page designer should strive for? Discuss and compare your thoughts with a friend.*

 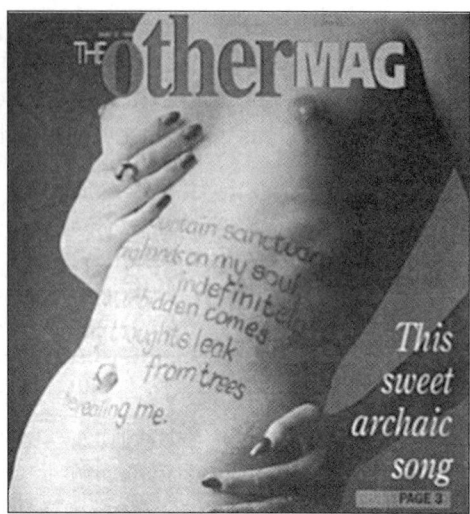

Typography

Typography is the foundation of newspaper design and strongly affects the look of a publication. There are thousands of typefaces or fonts available to designers. The typeface that a designer chooses should always be easy and pleasant to read. A fancy typeface may look good but might be very difficult to read.

Type terms

The following terms are commonly used to describe the parts and the qualities of typefaces. The examples below the definitions should help you.

Ascender   The part of a letter that rises above the x-height.
Bowl   The rounded stroke that creates an enclosed space.
Character   Individual figures, letters and punctuation marks.
Counter   The space enclosed within a character.
Descender   The part of a letter that falls below the baseline.
Families   All the sizes and typestyles (i.e. bold, medium, light, italic, condensed, expanded, etc.) of a particular typeface.
Font   A complete set of characters, i.e. lower- and upper-case characters, figures and punctuation marks.

Lowercase	Small letters are called *lowercase characters*, as in 'a' below.
Serif	The lines that make the ears, feet or tails on the main strokes of a character. Serifs make type easier to read.
Uppercase	Capital letters are called 'caps' or uppercase.
X-height	The vertical height of a letter, excluding ascenders and descenders.

Fonts

Fonts are divided into several main categories:

Serif (Roman): These typefaces, also called Roman, have serifs or little finishing strokes at the end of the stems, arms and tails of characters. Serifs make type easier to read. Examples of Roman type include Times, used here, Garamond, Courier and Goudy.

> TIMES is an example of a Roman face. This paragraph has been set in 12 point Times Roman.

> GARAMOND is an example of a Roman face. This paragraph has been set in 12 point Garamond.

Sans serif: Sans serif typefaces also known as *Gothic*, do not have serifs (*sans* is French for *without*). Serif typefaces have strokes that are the same thickness throughout. Examples include Futura, Franklin Gothic, Helvetic, Impact and Univers.

> **Impact is an example of a sans serif face. This paragraph has been set in 10 point.**

> **HELVETICA** is an example of a sans serif face. This paragraph has been set in 10 point Helvetica Medium.

Cursive: Cursive typefaces (also called script), resemble formal handwriting. Most script typefaces are not easy to read and should be used judiciously [with careful thought], if at all.

This paragraph has been set in 14 point Brush Script.

Type measurements and layout

Measuring type and layout is traditionally done in *points* and *picas.*

Points: Points are about the size of the mark made by a finely sharpened pencil. Points are used to measure small areas in a publication, like the height of type and the thickness of rules.
> 12 points equal 1 pica
> 72 points equal 1 inch, or 2.2 cm.

Picas: Often called *ems,* picas are used to measure larger areas in publications, such as the width and length of columns of type and in sizing photographs.
> 6 picas equal 1 inch, or 2.2 cm.

Kerning: Kerning refers to the space between individual letter pairs in a particular typeface family. Kerning is done to aid readability. Although when a typeface is supplied, the overall spacing of individual letters is satisfactory, the user may wish to change the spacing between some or all letter pairs to make the text easier to read or to give a distinctive [special] look to their publication. Letters that almost always require kerning are A, V, W, Y and all rounded letters. Today, computers allow for very precise spacing to meet the publication's need.

Tracking: Tracking as opposed to kerning is the *proportional* spacing between letters and words. In other words, the spacing between letters and words can be either increased or decreased by a set amount, almost like a concertina.
> ABabCDcd – normal , ABabCDcd – condensed,
> ABabCDcd – extended

Leading: Leading refers to the spacing between *lines*, which is normally set at 120% of the type size, (e.g. leading for 10pt type will be 12pt). Leading set in this way makes type easier to read.

Editing by design

Jan V White in his excellent book, *Editing by Design* says:

> "... there is more to creative magazine/newspaper
> editing than marking-up copy: by an aware use of
> expressive graphic element and a purposeful relationship
> of words and pictures, space becomes communication,
> not mere ornament." [52.]

Editors should aim to organise material in such a way that the
significance [the meaning] of the material shines through. But how
can an editor achieve this? Firstly, by choosing suitable words skilfully. Secondly, by organising facts and ideas into a logical
sequence so that the thought becomes clear and the tone [the way
of addressing the reader] convinces the reader. Lastly, the layout
should help a reader to *see* the editor's tone of voice through the
size and darkness of the text and the position of the text in the
publication. Words or text are the editor's *verbal* tools. Everything
else is a *visual* tool.

Working with visual elements

Photographs, pictures and illustrations are all *visual elements* and
can be edited in the same way as words are edited. So, how do
we edit visual elements? Well, firstly, choose the right visual elements,
just as you would choose suitable words. Then arrange them in a
sequence that strengthens the 'word message' that your visual instrument is illustrating. Use size and visual emphasis (refer to examples
on pages 200 and 202) to show the level of importance of the
material. This is done just as we use tone of voice when we speak.
It is therefore important that the editor and the designer understand
each other and what they are trying to achieve. They must always
be aware of the close relationship between the text and visual
elements and remember that neither text nor visual elements can
work well without the other. The end result must be an interesting,
memorable product that can be read quickly and absorbed easily.

Successful publications have their own style and character and do not see design as a decoration. They use design to interpret the meaning of an article so that the article comes alive for the reader.

Tabloid design

Spencer is quoted as saying that *"unread type is merely a lot of paper and a little ink".*

When we consider the costs and returns of printing newspapers we should not think only of how much has been produced. We need to consider *how much people have actually read and understood.*

The tabloid newspaper was designed so that millions of people *would* read and understand it. This was successful. Tabloids are one of the most efficient mass communication media invented so far. *The Sowetan* is an excellent example of a popular tabloid.

What is special about the design of the tabloid? It is designed so that readers can *scan* it easily, that is, look through quickly, seeking items that interest them. People don't give much time to reading newspapers nowadays. (This is partly because there are other news sources like radio and television.) They want something that they can read and also understand *quickly.*

Thus a successful tabloid generally aims at stories that are easy to read, not very long and set in a highly legible font. The page layout generally shows an attractive balance of text, headlines, photographs, illustrations and advertising.

Tabloid layout avoids too many different eye-catching features on one page. Small pictures balance large ones and white space is used so that each article stands out in an easy-to-read way.

The role of pictures in design

In early newspapers, there were very few pictures or none at all. Only one modern newspaper, the *Wall Street Journal* manages to ignore pictures. This is because it has developed an editorial style that makes it one of the great newspapers of all time.

Pictures are important to good design. We use them not only to provide information, but also to focus the reader's eye. Pictures form part of the basic design mix together with text, headlines and adverts. However, a newspaper page often has to be designed before the pictures that will be used are ready, because news coverage depends on the news of the day. The person designing the page must brief the photographer so that the photographer knows exactly what type of picture to take. This is an extremely important process, and sometimes compromises have to be made by designer, reporter or photographer.

We use the same method to select the right picture as we do to select the appropriate article. The following must be considered when we design a page:

Composition: The grouping and position of people (or other subjects of the picture) must be appealing.
Balance: The picture must balance with the rest of the page.
Quality: There must be plenty of contrast between dark and light.

A good rule is that if the main picture is supporting the page lead or the half lead then it must be integrated into the main text and the headline. It must be done in such a way that it also plays a part in the structure of the whole page.

Picture editing

The person who draws the page usually has the job of editing the pictures on it too. In some cases, this person is the sub-editor. The art editor would also wish to be involved in the selection of the appropriate picture. The main elements in picture editing are *briefing, cropping, scaling or sizing* and *retouching*.

Briefing the photographer

In order to get the best pictures, it is important to brief [instruct] the photographer to include certain details, angles, close-ups or people so that the pictures will suit specific layouts. One advantage of staff work [working as a staff team] is that there can be a detailed briefing when pictures are being planned as part of the contents of certain pages or features.

Another important factor to consider is the limitations and advantages of the modern digital camera. Most newspapers today are using digital cameras which allow the direct transfer of the image or photo by means of a laptop computer fitted with a cellular phone and modem. The advantage of this is that the image can be worked on immediately and dropped into the page. Time is no longer wasted in developing the picture.

An experienced photographer will shoot several different images to give the editor a number of layout choices. The editor will then have a choice if the shape of the advertising on the page changes, or if the story and pictures need to transfer to another page. Sometimes the opportunity for a great picture comes suddenly and unexpectedly. This could even change the focus or the angle of a story. An editor will always consider using a great picture, because pictures create interest and can sell newspapers.

Cropping

There are many editorial reasons for including and excluding certain detail from a picture. The reasons could relate to the amount of advertising on the page or to the most effective page design. Actually, few pictures get used in exactly their original form, and unwanted details are cut out or cropped. Pictures usually fill a functional role, to inform the reader. Do not use a picture only for artistic merit or because it is 'beautiful'. Your reader will not be fooled, and you could lose credibility which you have struggled to gain.

An important kind of cropping happens when we use only part of the picture and then blow up this part because we want to emphasise it. Some pictures on the other hand are cropped to improve their composition or to exclude people or things that are not relevant to the article that the picture is illustrating. Sometimes the only picture available is not a good one and cropping can improve its quality and usefulness.

Cropping should always serve editorial purpose and function, that is, it should help to convey the meaning of the story and fit in with the needs of the page layout. A picture that is very good from a photographer's point of view may not fit these demands. Ensure that you don't lose essential features during cropping, if you do, you could be accused of excluding this detail to mislead the reader and to misrepresent the situation.

Broadly speaking, a picture should be cropped when there is unnecessary and distracting background or unwanted detail to ensure that the relevant parts of the picture's subject form the main area.

Original picture.   Cropped picture.

Sizing/scaling

A big story usually demands a big picture and the layout staff have to make important decisions about how much prominence to give to a picture or pictures. Obviously, the bigger the picture the less space there will be for copy, as there is only a finite amount of space available on a page. When two or more pictures illustrate the same story, never make them the same size. One picture will always be closer to the central message of the story and should therefore be larger than the other one. The differentiation by size is one of editing's most effective techniques. Remember that something only seems 'big' because something else is smaller.

How do we go about sizing or scaling a picture? The size of pictures in the modern modular design always depends on the size of the columns and the number of columns per page. Nowadays pictures are not allowed to intrude across part of a column. Pictures must be sized according to the number of columns they will occupy, e.g. single column, double column, and so on.

There are two methods usually used to scale a picture.

Method 1:

1. Measure the height and width of the photo/picture you want to size.
2. Measure the width of the columns the picture must cover.
3. To calculate the new height of the picture proceed as follows:

Calculation

$$\frac{\text{height (actual picture)}}{\text{width (actual picture)}} = \frac{\textit{New height (unknown)}}{\text{Column(s) width (known)}}$$

therefore:

$$\frac{\text{height (actual picture)}}{\text{width (actual picture)}} \times \frac{\text{Column(s) width (known)}}{1}$$

$$= \textit{New height (unknown)}$$

Scaled to 60% of
original picture.

Scaled to 50%
of original.

Scaled to 40%
of original.

Method 2:

1. Decide on the picture width (that is, the number of columns to use) that suits the page.
2. Place a piece of tracing paper over the picture.
3. Draw a diagonal line on the tracing paper, across the picture from corner to corner.
4. Measure the required width along the base of the picture and then draw a perpendicular line from that point to the diagonal line.
5. From the point of intersection with the diagonal, draw a horizontal line which will give you the new height.

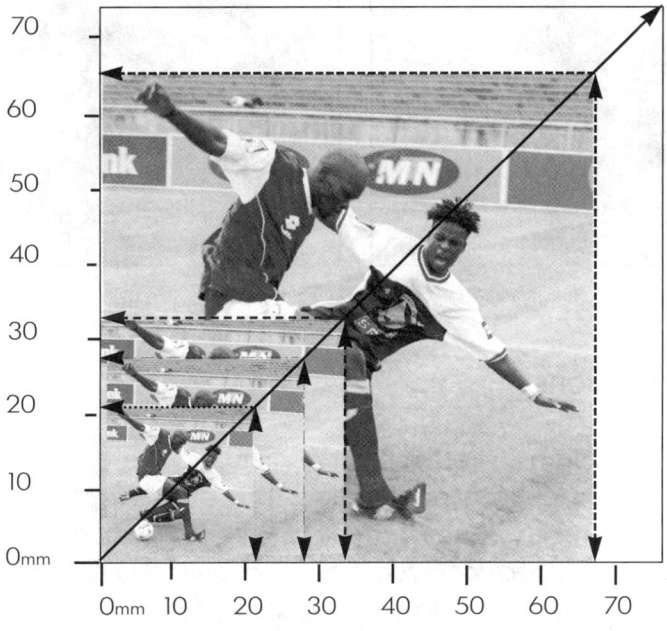

For both methods, you could find that after sizing, the new height is still too big for the space allocated by the editor. If this is so, the sized picture must be cropped again to obtain the correct size. However, today most sizing is done on screen by the person laying-out the page.

Retouching

Retouching is done to improve the quality of a picture and is an important part of picture editing. But retouching can be very controversial and you should therefore take care and thought if you do it. Retouching is usually done by specialists when the quality of a picture is not quite good enough. Good retouching should not be noticeable to the reader and the main aim should be to remove unwanted detail in the picture. Care must be taken that the essence [the main style and message] of the picture is not interfered with in any way. In the example below, can you see how the original picture has been altered?

Original picture.

Retouched picture.

Legal considerations

When either cropping or retouching a picture, take great care that the subject of the picture is not libelled. This even applies to animals. *A national daily was in trouble in the 1950s when an overzealous [overkeen] retoucher reduced the size of a prize bull's vital member and the owner, who relied on stud fees, sued.* [53.]

Selecting the right photographs

A good photograph is one that helps illustrate the point of the story. You may have more attractive and better composed pictures to choose from but the picture you choose should be the one that clearly defines, illustrates and articulates the point of the story. It is important to ensure that the photograph helps the reader understand the story. It must in no way confuse the reader or contradict the text. A good photograph will strengthen the story's argument [its main point(s)].

When selecting photographs, spread them all out in front of you so that you can judge them all at the same time and you will immediately be able to notice differences in quality, composition and focus. You can then start eliminating those photographs that are inappropriate to the story.

A reminder: do not be fooled into using 'pretty' pictures that do not enhance the story as you will lose credibility with your readers.

To sum up: there are a number of important considerations when selecting pictures.

Appropriateness: The picture must be appropriate to the story and this must always be your first requirement. Also, the picture must enhance and not merely repeat the story (most newspapers often make the latter mistake).

Impact: Does the picture grab the reader's attention? Does the reader want to find out the story behind the picture? The best pictures are always those that are out of the ordinary. Does the picture add to the creative dimension of the page?

Quality: Make sure that the picture you use is of the best quality. Pictures that are dull, grainy or out of focus create graphic 'noise' and therefore if these are all you have you should rather not use a picture.

Design possibilities: Because pictures play as big a part as the actual story and a vital part in the overall design, they must always be evaluated and edited for their design possibilities.

A boring picture does nothing to improve a boring page. A picture should either explain the story or grab the reader's attention. Good pictures can grab the reader's attention just as a good headline can. Headlines are written in big bold type specifically to attract the reader's attention. Pictures can be used to generate interest in the same way as headlines are used.

 Conclusion

To layout and design a publication effectively, you must understand the technicalities behind layout and design. Good layout and design is not haphazard [does not just happen as you go along]. They require discipline and knowledge. The modern journalist needs to know more and more about the layout and design of a publication. The journalist is very often required to lay out a story within an allocated space on a page. An understanding of the principles of design and layout is therefore essential.

Suggested Reading

1. Giles, Vic & Hodgson, F W, *Creative Newspaper Design*, Heineman, Oxford, 1990.

2. Nel, Francois, *Writing for the Media*, Southern Book Publishers, 1995.

3. White, Jan V, *Editing by Design*, R R Bowker Company, 2nd edition, New York, 1982.

Trade unions –
17   the freedom to associate

 # Introduction

Why should a journalist join a media union? This chapter looks at this question. It also offers a description and history of trade unionism in the South African media industry, including both the newspaper industry and the electronic media – radio and television.

 # Outcome

At the end of this chapter, you will know what a trade union is and why it is in your interest to join one. You will also have a basic understanding of the history of the two main media unions.

 # 5 Minute Task

> *Before you read on, consider:*
> *• Will you join a journalists' trade union or not?*
> *• What do you consider the advantages and/or disadvantages of joining a union?*
> *• Do you know which unions you could join? Which would you choose and why?*
> *• What have you heard about the other union(s), and what do you think about them?*
> *Respond to these questions yourself, and then also discuss them with a fellow-student, if possible. Then read on.*

Why join a union?

By now you probably have a picture of the special role that journalists play in society, we are the watchdogs, the conscience of the nation, the social commentators. As journalists, we work in a demanding and sometimes volatile [fast-changing] environment. Sometimes even our best efforts don't prevent mistakes occurring in our reports. Sometimes management deals with us in a high-handed [domineering, inconsiderate] and one-sided manner. Sometimes enemies of the free press attack us. At times like these, journalists need a union to protect their rights.

Around the world, journalists face common threats related to safety, working conditions, censorship laws, dictatorships, restriction of movement, and so on. Again, our unions can help us to respond to these threats from a stronger position.

Every journalist has the freedom to associate with whichever union he or she chooses. In South Africa, there are two main unions which deal with the rights of journalists. These two unions now work more in collaboration with one another than in opposition, although there is no strong single forum. It is in the interests of all journalists to join either the *South African Union of Journalists (SAUJ)* or the *Media Workers' Association of South Africa (MWASA)*.

Apartheid newsrooms

In South Africa, journalism has been a black and white issue. Journalists worked in the same medium but lived in two different worlds. White journalists lived in safe suburbs and blacks (Africans, Indians and coloureds) in apartheid-zoned ghettos. While the whites were expected to reflect a 'normal' society at work and at play, black journalists had to witness an 'abnormal' society living in the terrible social conditions under apartheid.

To take the profession into the 21st century, we have to deal with the past. Since they entered the newspaper industry more than a hundred years ago, black media workers have struggled against apartheid laws and other obstacles to attain parity, respect and dignity. They have had to fight to oust racism from the industry and to get justice from their white management.

Under apartheid, black media workers were cut off from the mainstream working of the industry. Many were given the jobs of sweeping the floors, ferrying the copy and working on ethnic-based African, Indian and coloured *Extra* editions of the main paper. Basically, the typical South African newsroom was divided into two distinct groups – whites and blacks, privileged and oppressed.

White journalists were given the best jobs as editors, senior writers and chief photographers. Blacks were just 'extras' – they hunted for the stories in the townships and handed them to educated whites who would rewrite and alter the story in tune with the newspaper's editorial policy. Black journalists had second-class status in the media industry. Yet according to the traditions of this industry it should have been leading the lobby against institutionalised dis-crimination, racial injustice and human rights abuses.

Frustrated black journalists therefore started to form new groupings. The Union of Black Journalists was the first such group to appear, only to be banned under State President PW Botha's state of emer-gency. The emergency choked the rising tide of the black conscious-ness movement after the time of the Soweto Riots. Black journalists responded to the UBJ's banning by forming the *Writers' Association of South Africa (WASA)* in the late 70s.

At that time, a new breed of politically-conscious black journalists were starting their careers. Among them was Zwelakhe Sisulu, son of Walter Sisulu, jailed ANC secretary-general and lieutenant of Nelson Mandela.

Media Workers' Association of South Africa (MWASA)

Black journalists started to feel that they could no longer organise themselves exclusively in a professional group and WASA was short-lived. Journalists joined forces with the shop-floor workers, sweepers, messengers, drivers, machine-room operators, advertising representatives and other media workers. Together they launched the *Media Workers' Association of South Africa (MWASA)* in Cape Town in 1980.

Under Zwelakhe Sisulu's outspoken leadership, MWASA became a thorn in the flesh of the Anglo-American owned Argus Company. Since then there has been an unhappy, bitter relationship between union and management. MWASA had a fiery political birth. In 1980, only months after it arose as the first full union to challenge the industry, MWASA organised a national strike in which more than one thousand media workers downed tools. The strike lasted 13 weeks and badly disrupted newspaper production, news gathering and distribution. Many of the anti-apartheid forces and extra [outside] parliamentary organisations supported the strike action strongly.

Dennis Beckett, editor of the news magazine, *Frontline*, wrote in December 1980:

> *"In August this year, a small blacks-only trade union called the Writers Association of South Africa, orchestrated the first production-stopping strike in South African publishing history. The strike took 'Post', the Argus Company's African newspaper, off the streets for a week. It ended with the introduction of wage scales substantially higher than those on white papers."*

In October, 1980, WASA met in Cape Town for its annual congress and changed its name to the *Media Workers' Association of South Africa (MWASA)*. It severed what Beckett called its *"last lingering vestiges [scraps] of respect for the traditional ethic of objective journalism"*. What was this – a trade union or a mass movement?, asked Beckett.

Soon after the historic congress which united black media workers (reporters and labourers), white-collar workers at the *Cape Herald*, the Argus Company's coloured newspaper, went on strike in protest against poor pay and working conditions. Within a week, the majority of black journalists at *Argus* and *South African Associated Newspapers* (SAAN) walked out in sympathy and the *Post* was once more off the streets. MWASA was absolutely firm in its strike stance. It was determined to break the seemingly equally unmoving *Argus* and *SAAN* management. The union fought a tough battle for recognition and the reinstatement of all its dismissed journalists and workers. MWASA won both these, and so introduced a new challenge to the newspaper management. Eventually this developed into a culture of negotiation with employers who were previously reluctant to make deals. Historically, the South African Society of Journalists (SASJ) had not had much success in its dealings with a management that was basically resentful of any union types.

South African Union of Journalists (SAUJ)

What follows is an extract and summary from the submission of the South African Union of Journalists to the Truth and Reconciliation Commission, concerning the role of the media during the apartheid era. It was prepared by the President of the SAUJ, Sam Sole and delivered to the TRC on 11 June 1997.

The SAUJ represents more journalists (1400) – Black or White – than any other union in South Africa. It is an independent multiracial union, self-funded, and affiliated to the International Federation of Journalists.

Under apartheid, SAUJ was represented mainly in the commercial English language press. After 1960, the SAUJ lost the few members it had within the Afrikaans media. Management of the Afrikaans press intimidated these members into leaving the union. There were extreme political differences between the English language press, which was anti-apartheid, and the Afrikaans media, which supported the National Party.

The SAUJ operated mainly in the *Argus Group* newspapers (later *Independent Newspapers*), *South African Associated Newspapers* (later *Times Media Limited*), and an ever dwindling [decreasing] number of independents, such as the *Natal Witness* and the *Daily Dispatch*. More recently the SAUJ have had a branch at the *Weekly Mail* (later renamed the *Mail & Guardian*), and also at *Umafrika*. Now and then they have had members and sometimes also branches at other publications such as *South, Pace, Ilanga, Sowetan* and *City Press*.

Those large institutions where most of the SAUJ's members worked were tainted [affected, poisoned] by apartheid. The SAUJ did not function as a union for radicals or revolutionaries. According to Sole, we need to look at the SAUJ and the English language press and ask: *How hard did they challenge restrictions and prejudices for the sake of justice, human rights, press freedom, and the other ideals which journalists should strive for?* In short, we should judge the English press according to the same liberal ideals that it claims to hold.

A relevant history

The SAUJ was founded as the South African Society of Journalists (SASJ) in 1920, this makes it one of the oldest unions in the country. (The union changed its name in the 90s and SASJ and SAUJ are used interchangeably.) Like most institutions in South Africa at that time, the industry and the union were white. Although the Society was sup-posed to be open to all, there were no members of other races. Up until the late 1950s, the main issues were: *Should the Society remain a union or become a professional body?* and *How could the union bridge the gap between Afrikaans and English speaking journalists?*

The union first began to deal with the race issue in 1958 when the National Party introduced the Industrial Conciliation Act, which made the existence of completely mixed trade unions impossible. Under this act, a union that wished to remain mixed or to become mixed would be de-registered. It would then lose the protection of the labour legislation of that time.

Although the SASJ had no black members at that time, they wrote to the Minister to ask for an exemption from the requirements of the new Act. They had applicants for membership who were awaiting the out-come. However, the Minister dismissed this appeal as *'an audacity'*. To avoid being de-registered, the SASJ stayed within the requirements of the Act and members voted in 1960 for the *'partially mixed'* option in the Act. This option allowed a union to have coloured and Indian members in separate branches from the white members. However, these members were also not allowed to stand for the executive posi-tions of the Society. And African journalists were completely excluded by the Act. Some members resigned in protest at this decision.

1960 was, of course, the year of the Sharpeville massacre and *The Journalist*, the official journal of the union, reacted to the tragedy in its April 1960 edition. Under the headline *Sharpeville: is there an office censor now?* the writer condemned the inadequate press coverage of the massacre. In particular, he criticised the failure to use the shocking picture of dozens of scattered bodies of unarmed protesters mowed down when the police opened fire. He also slammed the mainstream papers conservative interpretation of the Emergency Regulations, which had been imposed soon after Sharpeville. However, although these views appeared on the front page of *The Journalist*, the article was accompanied on that page by a disclaimer which stated that it must not be taken to represent the opinions of the SASJ and *The Journalist*.

In the 70s came a resurgence [awakening, rising] of political activity. The Black Consciousness Movement arose, and English university campuses became more politicised. In the SASJ there was a campaign to get employers to offer black journalists equal opportunities for training and to introduce equal pay scales. The request fell on deaf ears. The sharp contrast between what pious editors preached and what editors actually practised was very clear.

In 1974 the union began to lobby to de-register, so that it could be opened up to all races. Three referendums were held before the SASJ achieved the two-thirds majority needed to dissolve the Society in 1977 and reconstitute *outside* the Industrial Conciliation Act. It was perhaps too little, too late. By that stage, the 1976 protests and the harsh action against black journalists and black newspapers had opened up a deep chasm between the SASJ and the black unions (the *Union of Black Journalists*, later the *Writers Association of South Africa* and, later still, the *Media Workers' Association of SA*).

This rift [break, division] unfortunately remains today. There has been much co-operation over the years. For example, SAUJ members in the print media held a picket at SABC in support of a MWASA dispute. Also, SAUJ and MWASA have co-operated in dealings with the International Federation of Journalists (IFJ). However, unions still lack the will to submerge their identities into one. Today the new Labour Relations Act, which is hostile to small unions like the SAUJ and MWASA, may well force greater formal co-operation. But it could also create destructive competition.

In the 1980s, one result of the State of Emergency was pressure on journalists in the SAUJ to come up with a clear response to the situation. One group pressured for the SAUJ to become politically aligned and another group asserted that the job of journalists is to be independent, not to be politically aligned.

The union resisted co-option by either side. That made things hard for the SAUJ sometimes, especially when dealing with foreign organisations which questioned why the SAUJ didn't align itself with the ANC. The SAUJ held the line with regard to the independence of journalists. That is a very important legacy. One does not uphold one's independence only in relation to those you *don't* agree with. It can be argued that in relating to governments, you should also uphold your independence from those you may actually agree with. This is necessary because at some future time you may not agree, and then it is important to be able to declare yourself without any constraint. This position held the core message of the media, which is that the media must be a 'watchdog'.

There is a need to find a balance between profitability and marketability on the one hand, and, on the other hand, the responsibilities the media carries as an important support of civil society in a democracy. This is no easy line to draw, as the closure of *New Nation* shows. It was a newspaper committed to *informing*, not merely entertaining its readers, but it could not survive. All agree that press freedom is important for democracy. Yet it is notable that the only newspapers to have survived to carry out that task – however imperfectly - are the commercial mainstream papers. The others – *South, New Nation, New African,* etc. – have not survived. The closure of *New Nation* by its black owners is a painful reminder that the commercial news media is a business. They need to make money to survive and to be sensitive to their markets.

At present there is a lack of strong, unified media institutions and forums for debate. Media institutions are still fragmented [broken up], especially on racial lines. On the union side, the SAUJ and MWASA and the SA Typographical Union compete for membership. The one-upmanship [competition only for the sake of competition] between them allows little space for these organisations to formulate policy or take action together. The Black Journalist Forum does have cross-over membership of SAUJ and MWASA but also causes further fragmentation. All these bodies are relatively weak and stretched and cannot deal very effectively with the many workplace and media policy issues which face them daily.

If we look back at the many laws enacted to restrict the flow of news in South Africa, they indicate that the media did play some opposition role. The laws were aimed at the black and English press and the foreign media. There is no doubt that the mainstream press should have done more. But it is worth quoting Allister Sparks:

"What some of our critics today seem to be suggesting is that we should have been kamikaze fighters – crashed the plane into the ship, gone out of business with a blaze of glory. I don't believe, still, that was our role – we took calculated risks."

Sam Sole ends the submission of the SAUJ to the Truth and Reconciliation Commission as follows:

"The bequest of journalists to the New South Africa is a free press and an institutional independence. But that independence needs to be earned again and again. It depends on a credibility which was too easily squandered in the past, leaving the industry in debt to the nation. We, as an industry and as a profession, need to work harder to repay that debt."

 5 Minute Task

Now that you have read about unions generally and the South African media unions in particular:

- Have your ideas about unions changed in any way? If yes, how have they changed?
- Have you any ideas about which union you would like to join? If so, why have you chosen this one?
- What should happen in the future concerning media unions in South Africa, in your opinion?

 Conclusion

In this chapter you learnt what a trade union is and why it is in your interest to join one. You now have a basic understanding of the history of the two main media unions and what they stand for.

The future –
18   where to from here?

Introduction

The only thing that is certain in journalism is change. The modern newsroom is very different from the newsrooms of the past. Journalists no longer sit at typewriters but at highly sophisticated computers. Because newspaper managers continually demand greater profits, I predict the following: newsrooms will get smaller, newspapers will rely on technology more and more, fewer journalists will be employed full-time and there will be more freelance journalists.

In this publication, I have already looked at some of the changes that computer technology has brought. As you know, this technology has enabled stories to pass from the journalist to the sub-editor and back to the journalist without any personal contact between them. Further, the introduction of laptop computers, modems and cellular telephones means that the modern journalist does not even have to report to the newsroom, saving the newspaper and the journalist time and money.

Although technology in the newsroom is changing continually, the reporter's role of news gathering and reporting will remain the same and will continue to be the core of the newspaper business.

Outcome

At the end of this chapter, it will be clear what is expected of the journalist of the future.

5 Minute Task

> *Now that you have read and learnt more about journalism and the way it has developed, what do you think the job will be like for the journalist of 2050? In what ways will the job probably have changed by then? In what ways will it probably be the same as it is now? Note down your ideas quickly and share them with a fellow-student, if possible.*

Internet: What is the Internet?

The Internet can be described as a worldwide network of computers. It holds enormous amounts of information that you can access through a personal computer (PC). Commercial companies known as *service providers* provide access to the Internet. The most exciting thing about the Internet is that you do not have to be a computer expert to access the enormous variety and volume of information that is available there.

One great advantage of the Internet is that it provides access to data worldwide and also allows you to communicate with others worldwide from your own PC via electronic mail (e-mail), discussion groups, on-line chatting and the numerous sites that make up the World Wide Web.

How worldwide is the Internet?

It is technically possible for anyone with a PC, modem and telephone to obtain access to the Internet via a service provider. But some countries have very few providers and limited coverage. Also the telephone system in some countries may not be sophisticated enough to give access to the Internet.

However, as soon as you are connected to the Internet, you are able to communicate 'live' with over 70 million users. You can also communicate by e-mail, subscribe to newsgroups and mailing lists, do on-line shopping and have access to electronic software, data, sound and pictures stored on computers at libraries, newspapers, universities, businesses, organisations and private users that make up the Internet. The list of what makes up the Internet is growing every day.

Will newspapers survive?

Will the newspaper survive? Yes, of course it will, but newspaper editors will have to be far more strategic in their approach [they will have to adapt to new situations and plan more flexibly and imaginatively]. They will need to be more sensitive to their audience. Those modern editors who want their newspapers to survive well into the new millennium, will have to consider how their competitors – in radio, TV, and other electronic media – present news to these audiences. If these editors view radio, TV and the electronic media as their competition then I predict that they won't survive. If they view the other forms of media as *complementary* [part of the whole picture], then they have a bright and successful future ahead of them.

What do I mean by *complementary?* I mean that newspapers will *complete and expand* the news being broadcast by the other forms of media. A newspaper can never compete with the broadcast media for speed and visual appeal. So, what can newspaper editors do to survive?

Newspaper editors must learn to give their audience what radio and TV can't give. That is, depth, different angles, broad coverage, intensive investigative reporting and above all, *the story behind the story.*

Changes in technology

Over the last twenty years it seems that the reporter's role has been overshadowed by the dramatic advances in technology. But it is important to remember that without the journalist to gather and write the news accurately, all the technology in the world would be useless. However the journalist who wishes to advance should welcome new technology, not resist it. When computers first displaced the loyal and trusty typewriter in newsrooms, many seasoned hacks [experienced journalists] refused to accept the change and then found that it was overtaking them.

Do not fight changes in technology. Changes like e-mail replacing the fax machine (which itself replaced the old telex machine) have made the job of the journalist easier. A modern journalist can use a laptop computer fitted with a modem and a cellphone to write a story and relay it directly to the newsroom or anywhere else in the world, from the scene of the story. Digital cameras have cut out the need for darkrooms and all the paraphernalia that goes with developing pictures. The journalist can send a picture anywhere in the world in a matter of seconds by computer. The transfer of news and pictures now takes seconds instead of hours.

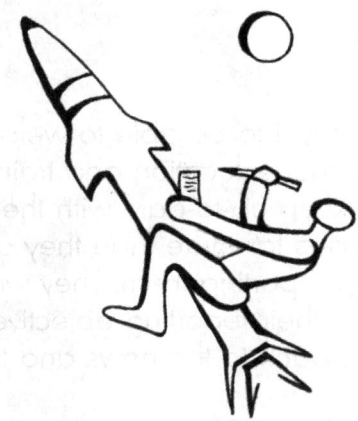

The journalist of the future

I believe that the journalist of the future will be able to do a number of jobs that they would not usually do now. Gaining this ability (formerly done by separate specialists) is called *multiskilling*. The journalist of the future will be able to take pictures, interview for broadcast and print, and be able to do features as well as hard news. The journalist of the future will also freelance for a number of media organisations and will probably specialise in a specific area of the news, like sport or crime.

But the basic *approach* of the journalist need not change much. Journalistic ethics, such as reporting truthfully and accurately, still apply. Although the Internet has brought some new sources of information to the journalist, news is still news. Information alone is not news. The journalist still needs to know sources and how to keep their local sources 'alive' and willing to supply the news. The journalist still needs to know how to use several sources for one story. The best journalists will use a range of sources and combine the information skilfully and critically. The Internet cannot think for the journalist. You, the journalist of the future, will still need to know how to analyse arguments and construct your own when you write stories.

Conclusion

Journalists of the future will need to be able to welcome change. They will continually seek further education and training in their area of speciality. They will keep up-to-date with the latest technology and they will use computers far more than they do now – both in researching stories and in reporting them. They will accept this as part of the way they achieve their reporting objectives. But they will still use the same basic approach to the news and they will still be guided by the same ethics.

Endnotes

1. Addison G, Rhodes Journalism Review, Vol13, Rhodes University, 1997, pp 34 - 36.
2. Ibid.
3. Ibid.
4. Nel, Francois, *Writing for the Media*, Southern Book Publishers, 1994, pp 197.
5. International Federation of Journalists Principles on the Conduct of Journalists.
6. Klaidman, Stephen, *et al*, *The Virtuous Journalist*, New York, Oxford University Press, 1987, pp 5.
7. Hulteng, John L, *Playing it Straight*, The Globe Pequot Press, Connecticut, 1981, pp 44.
8. The American Society of Newspaper Editors Statement of Principles, 1975, Article V Impartiality.
9. Klaidman, Stephen, *et al*, *The Virtuous Journalist*, pp 59.
10. Klaidman, Stephen, *et al*, *The Virtuous Journalist*, pp 126.
11. Klaidman, Stephen, *et al*, *The Virtuous Journalist*, pp 154.
12. Hulteng, John L, *et al*, *Playing it Straight*, pp 15.
13. Harriss, Julian, *et al*, *The Complete Reporter*, New York, MacMillan Publishing, 4th edition, 1981, pp 26.
14. Ibid.
15. Ibid.
16. Ibid.
17. Ibid.
18. Berry, Thomas Elliot, *Journalism in America*, New York, Hasting House Publishers, 1976, pp 27.
19. Brooks, Brian S, *et al*, The Missouri Group, *News Reporting & Writing*, New York, St Martins Press, 4th edition, 1992, pp 5.
20. Ward, Hiley H, *Professional Newswriting*, New York, Harcourt Brace Jovanovich Publishers, 1985, pp15.
21. Brooks, Brian S, *et al*, The Missouri Group, *News Reporting & Writing*, New York, St Martins Press, 4th edition, 1992, pp 12.
22. Teel, Leonard R, *et al*, *Into the Newsroom – An introduction to journalism*, Prentice-Hall, 1983, pp 97.
23. Abel, Elie, *Leaking: Who does it? Who benefits? At what cost?*, New York, Priority Press Publication, 1987.
24. Serafini, Anthony, *Philosophy and Journalistic Education; Philosophical Issues in Journalism*, Oxford University Press, New York, 1992, pp 252.
25. Brooks, Brian S, *et al*, The Missouri Group, pp 99.
26. Nel, Francois, *et al*, pp 72.
27. Ibid.

28. Lucas M. Oosthuizen, *Introduction to Communication*, Juta, 1996, pp 178.
29. Ibid.
30. Harris, Geoffrey, *Journalism Media Manual – Practical Newspaper Reporting*, 2nd ed, Focal Press, 1993, pp 77.
31. Spencer, Herbert, *The Invisible Word, Creative Newspaper Design*, 1986.
32. Brooks, Brian S, *et al*, pp 76.
33. Ibid, pp 84.
34. Ibid, pp 86.
35. Murray, Donald, *Writing for your Readers*, Connecticut, The Globe Pequot Press, 2nd edition, 1992, pp 12.
36. Brooks, Brian S, *et al*, pp 90.
37. Teel, Leonard R, *et al*, pp 156.
38. Crwys-Williams, Jennifer, *Dictionary of South African Quotations*, Penguin Books, Johannesburg, 1994, pp 332.
39. Ibid, pp 331.
40. Ibid, pp 339.
41. Nel, Francois, *et al*, pp. 149.
42. Brooks, Brian S, *et al*, pp 357.
43. Harriss, Julian, *et al*, pp 333.
44. Altschull, Herbert J, *Agents of Power*, Longman, New York, 1984, pp 202.
45. Ibid, pp 203.
46. Jackson, Gordon S, *Breaking Story – The South African Press*, Westview Press, Boulder, 1993, p 71.
47. Jackson, Gordon S, *et al*, pp 218.
48. Altschull, Herbert J, *et al*, pp 302 - 303.
49. Ibid, pp 151.
50. Ibid, pp 174.
51. Ibid, pp 174.
52. White, Jan V, *Editing by Design*, R R Bowker Company, 2nd edition, New York, 1982, pp 4.
53. Giles, Vic, & Hodgson, F W, *Creative Newspaper Design*, Heineman, Oxford, 1990, pp 89.